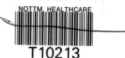
# Asylum to Action

*Community, Culture and Change*
*(formerly Therapeutic Communities)*

Series editors: Rex Haigh and Jan Lees

Community, Culture and Change encompasses a wide range of ideas and theoretical models related to communities and cultures as a whole, embracing key Therapeutic Community concepts such as collective responsibility, citizenship and empowerment, as well as multidisciplinary ways of working and the social origins of distress. The ways in which our social and therapeutic worlds are changing is illustrated by the innovative and creative work described in these books.

*other books in the series*

**Setting Up New Services in the NHS**
**'Just Add Water!'**
*Community, Culture and Change 13*
Kingsley Norton
ISBN 1 84310 162 9

**Therapeutic Communities**
**Past, Present and Future**
*Community, Culture and Change 2*
Edited by Penelope Campling and Rex Haigh
Foreword by John Cox
ISBN 1 85302 626 3

**A Culture of Enquiry**
**Research Evidence and the Therapeutic Community**
*Community, Culture and Change 6*
Edited by Jan Lees, Nick Manning, Diana Menzies
and Nicola Morant
ISBN 1 85302 857 6

**Dangerous and Severe – Process, Programme**
**and Person**
**Grendon's Work**
*Community, Culture and Change 15*
Mark Morris
ISBN 1 84310 226 9

**Therapeutic Approaches in Work with Traumatized**
**Children and Young People**
**Theory and Practice**
*Community, Culture and Change 14*
Patrick Tomlinson
Foreword by Paul van Heeswyk
ISBN 1 84310 187 4

# Asylum to Action

## Paddington Day Hospital, Therapeutic Communities and Beyond

*Helen Spandler*

*Community, Culture and Change 16*

Jessica Kingsley Publishers
London and Philadelphia

Words and music by Leonard Cohen on p.32 and p.55 taken from 'Bird on a Wire' from *Songs From a Room* (1969) © 1969 Stranger Music Inc. Sony/ATV. Reproduced with permission.

First published in 2006
by Jessica Kingsley Publishers
116 Pentonville Road
London N1 9JB, UK
and
400 Market Street, Suite 400
Philadelphia, PA 19106, USA

*www.jkp.com*

**Library of Congress Cataloging in Publication Data**
Spandler, Helen, 1969-
Asylum to action : Paddington Day Hospital, therapeutic communities, and beyond / Helen Spandler.
p. cm. -- (Community, culture, and change ; 16)
Includes bibliographical references and index.
ISBN-13: 978-1-84310-348-6 (pbk. : alk. paper) ISBN-10: 1-84310-348-6 (pbk. : alk. paper)
1. Paddington Day Hospital--History. 2. Therapeutic communities
--England--London--History--Case studies.  I. Title. II. Series.
[DNLM: 1. Paddington Day Hospital. 2. Hospitals, Psychiatric
--history--London. 3. Milieu Therapy--history--London. 4. Therapeutic
Community--London.   WM 28 FE5 S735a 2006]
RC489.T67S63 2006
362.2'109421--dc22
                                                    2005026418
**British Library Cataloguing in Publication Data**
A CIP catalogue record for this book is available from the British Library

ISBN-13: 978 1 84310 348 6
ISBN-10: 1 84310 348 6

Printed and bound in Great Britain by
Athenaeum Press, Gateshead, Tyne and Wear

Kenneth J. Spandler 1932–2003

# *Acknowledgements*

First, I would like to acknowledge some of the key players in this story whose work helped inspire my interest and research into Paddington Day Hospital, most notably Julian Goodburn, Trish Thomas, Liz Davies, Brian Douieb and Mike Lawson.

Erica Burman was consistently supportive and informative during the arduous process of writing up the PhD thesis on which this book is based. Mark Cresswell, Alec Jenner, Ian Parker, Jenny Secker and Jeremy Spandler also helped enormously by spending time reading through previous drafts of this book and giving invaluable, positive and detailed comments.

I would like to thank Bob Hinshelwood for encouraging me to write this book. Craig Fees and the Planned Environment Therapy Trust Archive and Study Centre (PETTS) provided access to their wonderful archive, help with transcriptions and a donation to help with travel costs. The Higher Education Funding Council for England (HEFCE) and the Department of Psychology and Speech Pathology at Manchester Metropolitan University provided research funding, and the Discourse Unit at MMU continues to be a valuable space for critical enquiry.

Conversations and contact with many other people helped my research in lots of different ways. They include: Claire Baron, Janet Batsleer, David Brandon, David Clark, Richard Crocket, Peter Campbell, John Davison, Tim Durkin, Rachel Foakes, Brian Haddon, John Hopton, Natasha Jenner, Rachel Jukes, Carolyn Kagan, Kath Knowles, Lionel Kreeger, Rebecca Lawthom, Marion Lindsay, Lesley Lougher, Louise Pembroke, Andrew Roberts, Ruth Rosen, Nicky Stanley, Carol Tindall, Stephen Ticktin, William West, Bill Williams and the Manchester Mental Patient's Union (MPU).

Finally, a very special mention must go to Meg Allen for really helping me to carve a book out of an unwieldy PhD thesis, asking those awkward questions and much more besides.

# Contents

# Preface

This book draws upon a variety of documents, together with interviews that I undertook as part of research about the protest and events at Paddington Day Hospital (Spandler 2002). Various participants in these events had kept related notes and documents, which I have drawn upon in developing my account. For example, Liz Davies and Brian Douieb kept material and notes relating to the campaign to save Paddington Day Hospital and the formation of the Mental Patients Union; Ismond Rosen had kept minutes of meetings relating to the Paddington Centre for Psychotherapy and the Day Hospital; and Richard Crocket had recorded his thoughts and reflections upon arriving at the day hospital after Julian Goodburn, the Medical Director in charge of the day hospital at Paddington at that time, was suspended. Because of the unofficial nature of these sources it is not possible to reference them in the usual way. However, since I have completed this research, the documentation kept by Richard Crocket has now been archived in the Planned Environment Therapy Trust Archives and Ismond Rosen's papers will be archived in the Wellcome Library for the History and Understanding of Medicine.

Other participants were able to take part in recorded interviews and, wherever possible, they are credited with their comments as direct quotations. These include: Julian Goodburn (Consultant/Medical Director), Trish Thomas (staff member), Liz Davies, formerly Durkin (student and co-ordinator of the campaign to save Paddington Day Hospital), Brian Douieb (activist and founder member of the MPU), Natasha Jenner, formerly Tavoosi (staff member), Mike Lawson (patient and MPU member), Lesley Lougher, formerly Mitchell (staff member and founder member of the MPU), Richard Crocket, and one staff member who wished to remain anonymous. I benefited from numerous conversations with various people involved either directly, or indirectly, in the events at Paddington Day Hospital, many of whom are listed in the acknowledgments.

In the rest of this book I will refer to Paddington Day Hospital in short-hand simply as 'Paddington'. In part, this is because it makes it easier to read but it is also because many of the people I interviewed used this term. In addition, although it is more customary in the modern context to use other terms such as 'mental health service users', I also use the term 'patients', because this was the term used at the time and that was adopted by the Mental Patients Union. It is perhaps paradoxical, given the radical approach that was developed at Paddington, that people who attended were referred to as such, since the term 'patients' implies a degree of medicalisation and passivity.

The research I undertook was broadly 'critical' in perspective, a term used in psychiatry and psychology to describe approaches that question the underlying assumptions and values of their respective disciplines. My research drew upon classical oral history methods, which helped to people my narrative since histories are personal, individual and collective. Indeed, at times the research process felt more like investigative journalism than more conventional methodologies. This was most apparent in the effort to track down Paddington participants. When I did manage to trace people, most were keen to review their experiences and get their particular angle on events heard. Many thought these events should be written up. I have been painfully aware in writing this book that it will not satisfy all the various, and often conflicting, perspectives that people held. I have developed my own perspective from a partial and limited position of never having been involved at the events at Paddington. Inevitably, many of the participants would not have necessarily fully endorsed my account. However, I hope that it does some justice to the complex, difficult and sometimes inspiring set of events at Paddington.

I started this research in 1999 but unfortunately, by the time I had completed it, a number of important figures in this history died. Most significantly, Julian Goodburn died unexpectedly in August 2001. In addition, David Brandon (an outspoken critic of therapeutic communities); Robert Hobson (author of *The Messianic Community*) and Robin Cooper (an important critic of the current regulation of therapeutic communities) all died during the period in which I carried out this research. Other key people in the Paddington events had already died before I embarked on this research. They include Svetlana Ilieva (staff member), Ismond Rosen (Chair of the Paddington Centre) and Eric Irwin (Paddington patient and founder of the Mental Patients Union). This only serves to underline the importance of trying to record accounts of important events in our modern history so that we can take advantage of collective memories even after the loss of important pioneers and activists.

The sad event of Julian Goodburn's sudden and premature death prevented me from being able to discuss these ideas any further with him but I hope that this testimony honours his work in ways he would have appreciated. Perhaps it might continue the honourable tradition taken forward by Peter Sedgwick, another important figure who was prematurely lost to us.

Peter wrote a highly valuable book called *Psychopolitics* (Sedgwick 1982) and was, reputedly, one of the few critics that R.D. Laing respected (Mullan 1995).

One of the inspirations for my research into Paddington was an article written by Liz Durkin in which she explicitly linked 'patient power' (which eventually led to the formation of the Mental Patients Union) with the particular therapeutic community practice developed at Paddington (Durkin 1972a). It was realising that this therapeutic community was also the subject of Claire Baron's damning critique *Asylum to Anarchy* (Baron 1987) which led me to a serious consideration of the story of Paddington. These two accounts seemed to illustrate both the best and worst in therapeutic community practices. This book is an attempt at both a celebration of the social action at Paddington as well as a sober reflection on, and critique of, *Asylum to Anarchy*. It is for this reason that I have called this book *Asylum to Action*.

# CHAPTER ONE

# Introduction and Context

There is a vast body of literature covering the history of therapeutic communities (TCs) as a whole, a wide-ranging subject area encompassing a broad range of disciplines and approaches that have existed and evolved over many years. This wider history is beyond the scope of this book, which concerns a modern history of therapeutic communities in the field of mental health and psychiatry (or anti-psychiatry). This book forms part of a process of historical recovery, contributing to a body of literature which documents innovation, debate and political struggles in psychiatry since the 1960s. The action and conflicts described here were innovative in that the mental health arena had not previously been seen as a collective forum for political struggle. In addition, it was 'prefigurative' of later social movements, including the emerging service user movement, which went on to explore in greater depth the notion of the personal as political.

Drawing on a variety of original sources, including oral history interviews and official as well as unofficial archival material, this book documents and analyses a number of events in the life of Paddington Day Hospital, a therapeutic community that was developed in West London, England, during the late 1960s and 1970s. It highlights particular moments of innovation and tries to recall some of the radical aspirations of therapeutic communities and the history of patients' activism. However, it also documents the difficulties and conflicts thrown up by these aspirations and argues that serious attention to such conflicts is still necessary in the search for more democratic and innovative mental health practices.

While many TCs themselves have survived in the face of wider political, economic and psychiatric changes, the concept and application of TCs as organisations that embody a radical spirit and force has declined. Russell Jacoby has called the process by which the radical impetus behind innovative ideas is forgotten or repressed a kind of 'social amnesia' (Jacoby 1975). If the radical potential of TCs has been forgotten, this is a fate that has also structured the history of psychoanalysis. Jacoby argued that hopes and commitments were buried and their visionary 'spirit and culture vaporised' (Jacoby 1983, p.7). There has always been a strand of progressive radicalised psychoanalysis which seeks both to find a wider political use for psychoanalysis and to use psychoanalysis to answer political questions, although such endeavours have usually been marginalised within the broader psychoanalytic movement. However, Jacoby has referred to a significant period in its history when psychoanalysis constituted part of a wider political project. He gives the example of the second generation 'political Freudians', clustered around Otto Fenichel from the 1920s until Hitler's rise to power in 1933 (Jacoby 1983). By the 1960s when the wider political culture had shifted there were re-newed attempts to re-radicalise psychoanalysis using, for example, Reich's Libertarianism.

This book is an attempt to redress this tendency in the history of TCs. I have tried to recapture some of the hopes, aspirations and radicalism of the therapeutic community movement through the story of Paddington. In order to put my story in context, (but without laying claim to a definitive history), I will, in two following sections in this chapter, review the trajectory of, and re-lationship between, three broader 'social movements': the therapeutic community movement, anti-psychiatry and the mental patients' (or service users') movement. I will then explain the importance of the history of Paddington Day Hospital within these developments before outlining the contents of the later chapters in this book.

## The therapeutic community movement and anti-psychiatry

There have been many attempts both to define therapeutic communities (Clark 1965; Haigh 1999; Kennard 1994; Kennard 1998; Rapoport 1960; Winship and Haigh 2000; Zeitlyn 1967) and to identify the potent and nec-essary ingredients in a TC (Haigh 1999; Kennard 1998; Rapoport 1960). The events and analyses of Paddington contributed to this debate, such that some commentators even concluded as a result that the TC itself was untena-ble (Cooklin 1981; Lemlij, Mulvany and Nagle 1982). However, in the UK at least, two ideas in particular gripped the imagination of TC pioneers: participative democracy and psychoanalysis (Kennard 1998). Similarly, it has been argued that the two key goals for TCs have been collective democratisa-tion and the creation of an optimal psychotherapeutic climate (Ahlin 1981).

In many ways this book reconsiders the intersection and dynamic between these ideas and practices through one important case study. It explores the constraints and opportunities encountered in TC initiatives that attempt to apply psychoanalytic ideas *and* practices of democratisation. Paddington Day Hospital illustrates important ongoing concerns that are at the heart of attempts to develop 'alternative' or 'radical' mental health practices, and the conflicts between therapeutic and political ideals.

Particular points in modern Western history have provided the social space in which therapeutic communities, or the 'therapeutic community impulse' (Kennard 1991), have been developed or re-ignited. On the one hand TCs can be viewed as another expansionist treatment technique in the growing armoury of the emerging technicians of mental health. The mental health industry has been seen as 'expansionist' in that it draws more and more aspects of our emotional and behavioural life within the remit of the psychiatric or psychological professions to control and regulate (Castel et al. 1982; Rose 1986). In this way, TCs can be seen as contributing to the broader ascendancy of the 'psy' disciplines as the new moral guardians of the psyche. Yet at the same time, TCs have also been viewed as a progressive, non-medicalised, anti-institutional (even anti-psychiatric) collectivised alternative to traditional hospital-based psychiatry.

In both spirit and history, the TC movement has been connected with the history of the development of psychoanalysis. Parker argued that psychoanalysis 'often seems to trace its way along a knife edge of conformity and revolutionary critique' (1997, p.14), carrying 'the most progressive as well as the most dubious elements of the enlightenment through modern culture' (p.250). This simultaneously positions psychoanalysis at both the more radical and the conformist ends of the mental health spectrum. Similarly, the history of TCs can be traced to specific responses to the dominant social forces and counter-forces of the time. While TCs attempt to collectivise distress and empower their members, they have also been intimately connected with the social, economic and cultural needs of the wider social order.

There are complex links between treatment technologies, the political conditions of their emergence and utilisation, their objectives and consequences (Rose 1986). 'Regulation theory' (Martin 2001) posits that historical periods require two essential elements – a regime of capital accumulation and a mode of social regulation – in order to ensure this accumulation. This mode of regulation consists of institutional forms and social relations. In this way, TCs can be viewed as being incorporated into normalising contemporary modes of regulation. In many ways TCs provide an ideal social-regulatory system in Western liberal-capitalist society, which requires the management, surveillance and treatment of the socially maladjusted and the transformation of attitudes to authority and the development of a functional efficiency (Castel *et al.* 1982; Rose 1986).

This was most evident in the role TCs played during World War II, providing both rehabilitated soldiers for the war effort and an efficient workforce for the expanding labour market in the post-war period. The ethics of TCs providing these broader economic and political functions can, of course, be questioned (see, for example, Margison 1992). For example, following Maxwell Jones' successful group work approach to rehabilitating soldiers suffering from what was known as 'effort syndrome', the Ministry of Labour gave him charge of the Industrial Neurosis Unit at the Belmont Hospital to rehabilitate the chronically unemployed, 'social misfits' (Whiteley 1979) or 'drifters' (Campling 2001). Maxwell Jones is one of the key figures in the history of TCs and it was here, during the 1950s, that he established what is now widely known as the 'therapeutic community'. In 1958 the Belmont was renamed the Henderson Hospital and has become the best-known established TC in the UK. The post-war situation of high employment and a corresponding increased demand for labour spawned a new therapeutic energy and optimism and this also fed into a renewed interest in social-rehabilitative psychiatry (Warner 1994). At the same time, the TC movement was being developed as a more humane and collective-based approach to the particular individualised and psychologised problems of our time. The assumption that a 'radicalised' mental health agenda equates with a 'social' or collective approach meant that the therapeutic community – social psychiatry's 'brightest star' (Rapoport 1960) – was ripe for an emerging radical mental health agenda. While this assumption is not without its critics and is by no means unproblematic (Donnelly 1992; Rose 1986), it is one that informs my research and is a fundamental principle of TCs (Tucker 2000).

In particular, the growing critique of psychiatry provided a fertile environment for the growth of TCs as an alternative to traditional, hospital-based psychiatric treatment. Dissatisfied with traditional psychiatric intervention, pioneers of the therapeutic community movement wanted radically to reform psychiatry and so attempted to provide a 'living learning' environment – a context of opportunity through which people could attempt to understand themselves and each other in a uniquely organised social milieu. TCs were held up as a response to a political and moral critique of modern psychiatry and they attracted interest and favour as a progressive alternative to traditional bio-medical hospital psychiatry. TCs advocated 'opening the doors' of the institutions and generally tolerated a great deal more psychic disturbance than was traditionally tolerated without resort to suppression with psychiatric drugs.

The expansion of radical movements and thinking during the late 1960s and early 1970s created another particular 'social space' in which the therapeutic community developed. The prevalent radical counter-culture of post-1968, and the innovators who both influenced and were influenced by it, emphasised and developed the more progressive tendencies in TCs. It was within this specific context that Paddington developed. TCs reflected, and were informed by, more general radical ideas such as communal living, experimentation, egalitarianism and anti-authoritarian forms of social organisation. This counter-cultural climate of experimentation and innovation helped support the toleration and expression of a greater degree of madness or disturbance. Such elements fitted the emerging concept of TCs and also helped to radicalise the concept of TCs themselves.

During this time there was an intense and productive cross-fertilisation of ideas and practices. The pioneers of 'anti-psychiatry' were drawn towards and developed TC ideas and practices as part of their radical agenda, particularly in the United Kingdom – turning the 'anti-psychiatry' TCs into another 'wing' of TC practice (Coppock and Hopton 2000). These are now seen as part of the history and roots of the TC movement (Kennard 1998; Tucker 2000). The most notable examples of such pioneering projects include Kingsley Hall (Barnes and Berke 1971; Barnes and Scott 1989; Burston 1996; Crossley 1999b; Laing 1968) and Villa 21 (Cooper 1965, 1967). Both Maxwell Jones and Tom Main, who are considered the two 'founders' of the therapeutic community approach, were on the initial advisory panel in 1965 that set up Kingsley Hall (Mullan 1995). In the context of group analysis (which has greatly informed TC practice), Laing's first article concerned an account of an analytic group in that tradition (Laing and Esterson 1958).

The convergence between anti-psychiatry and TCs could also be noted in other parts of Europe. Like the British anti-psychiatrists, the movement for democratic psychiatry (*Psichiatria Democratica*) in Trieste and Gorizia in Italy, grew out of, and developed, therapeutic community-type social psychiatry (Basaglia 1985, 1987; Donnelly 1992; Ramon 1988, 1989; Scheper-Hughes and Lovell 1987). For example, Franco Basaglia, the key theorist of Psichiatria Democratica in the early 1960s, instructed new colleagues to read key texts by Maxwell Jones about therapeutic communities (Donnelly 1992; Giannichedda 1989). A few years later in Germany, the Socialist Patients' Collective (SPK), which was formed in 1970, arose out of practices developed at Heidelberg Day Hospital (Kotowicz 1997; Spandler 1992). Although there were no explicit links with TCs, the work begun at Heidelberg resembled, at least initially, some of the TC practices being developed in the UK.

The particular paths that anti-psychiatry projects took in different countries clearly reflected the specific socio-political contexts in which they were conceived and developed. These reflected the strengths and weaknesses of particular more general counter-cultural political organisations and ideas that were being forged. Kotowicz (1997) argues that while the German SPK reflected the specific direct action strategies developed by the Baader Meinhof Group and the Red Army Fraction, Psichiatria Democratica reflected the strength of the Communist Party, which enabled far-reaching legal changes. Anti-psychiatry in the UK reflected the growth of the independent charitable sector during the 1970s when many radical initiatives developed. However, in terms of TCs, while Kingsley Hall was set up by an independent non-statutory organisation, the Philadelphia Association and other initiatives such as Villa 21 and Paddington were both developed in an NHS setting and this context may have constrained their development.

Perhaps it is mistaken to view the TC concept itself as having been the impetus for psychiatric reforms and oppositional strategies. Perhaps, rather, the TC at that time 'fitted', and was moulded to, the prevailing balance of dominant and alternative cultures, formations and forces. The 'therapeutic community impulse' can be viewed as forming part of a more general social-change momentum that specifically arose in opposition to the dominance of more custodial, institutionalised and medicalised psychiatric regimes. Indeed, many revolutionaries and social reformers have been attracted to TCs. For example, Sedgwick (1982) identified a left tradition of active social psychiatry, allied with militant tendencies of social reform. Some have made comparisons between an explicitly socialist approach to mental health and the democratic therapeutic community model (Mitchie 1980). Indeed, it does appear, at least taking a cursory glance, that therapeutic community-type environments may emerge following periods of intense and sustained progressive social change. In Cuba, following the 1959 revolution, mental health workers rejected prison-like conditions for psychiatric patients and created centres on therapeutic community lines (see Kennard 1991, p.37; Mitchie 1980, p.93). In addition, 'something very like' a TC developed in the aftermath of the Russian revolution (Kennard 1991, p.37).

However, while the anti-psychiatry pioneers were highly influenced by the TC concept and considered it to be a huge step forward, they were frequently disappointed with what they saw when visiting TCs – for example, the control exercised by staff (Claytor 1993). While many of the TCs in hospital wards and NHS residential settings primarily focused on therapeutic intervention and rehabilitation, the anti-psychiatric TCs were conscious attempts to put more radical ideas into practice and this meant linking their analysis to debates about social and political values (Kennard 1998). Although the emerging therapeutic community pioneers were in turn heavily influenced by anti-psychiatry and considered it as an important 'touchstone' in the development of TCs in the UK (Kennard 1998, p.101), the more political principles that informed these initiatives are now less of an overt influence on modern TCs. We can still see traces of this influence and legacy; but these are usually confined to people's autobiographical references about their own personal development rather than being a sustained and concrete influence on practice (Campling and Haigh 1999; Kennard 1998).

There still remains some tangible legacy of the relationship between the anti-psychiatric movement and TCs. For example, both the Philadelphia Association (which set up Kingsley Hall) and the Arbours Association set up by Joseph Berke are still in existence. In America during the 1970s Loren Mosher set up Soteria House dubbed the 'second generation Kingsley Hall' after being inspired by his brief stay at Kingsley Hall (Mosher 1991a, p.48). Although Soteria House was later forced to close, other similar initiatives have been set up in Europe such as Soteria Berne, which was established by the psychiatrist Luc Ciompi in Berne, Switzerland. Despite positive outcome research in relation to Soteria House, and the continued interest in such initiatives, their presence within the landscape of mental health provision continues to be sparse.

The Philadelphia Association has moved further into philosophical critique and deeper into psychoanalytical practice rather than providing practical social and political analysis (Cooper et al. 1994, Crossley 1998). Nevertheless, some still regard organisations such as the Philadelphia Association as 'social movement organisations', whose activity establishes mechanisms that keep the anti-psychiatric impetus alive (Crossley 1999b).

Received psychiatric wisdom regards these more radical initiatives as ultimately having failed and as merely a product of hedonistic, permissive times – therefore effectively writing them off. As a result there is little acknowledgement of some of the benefits, or any serious consideration of some of the limitations, of such radical attempts (Burston 1996). Notable exceptions do, however, challenge these conceptions. Thus Pullen has argued that Villa 21 was more than a 'failed experiment' and actually could offer much that is still useful (Pullen 1999). The lack of serious consideration of these alternatives is not just about 'evidence'. Despite the favourable outcome of recent research into Soteria House (Mosher 1991b; Mosher et al. 1995) there has been remarkably little interest in it, and this has been described as a 'deliberate neglect' (Burston 1996, p.149).

In Italy the democratic psychiatry movement is widely considered to have been an important innovation although its particular benefits and difficulties are highly contested within psychiatry (Ramon 1988, 1989). However, like the British anti-psychiatrists, this movement was keen to go beyond a confining model of clinical and professional practice. In particular, its pioneers criticised TCs as creating 'comfortable havens' in which inmates would still be effectively imprisoned, but against which they might be less inclined to rebel (Donnelly 1992, p.46). They began to realise that while TCs encouraged patients to fit into the wider social milieu, they didn't challenge that milieu. They envisaged the TC as a 'powerful means of unleashing new and dynamic interpersonal relations' (Donnelly 1992, p.45) rather than merely a therapeutic and rehabilitative tool.

Key theorists in Psichiatria Democratica were wary of just developing another fixed and unchanging 'technical model' of treatment or social administration designed to modify how the institution was run (Basaglia 1987, p.83). They challenged the tendency in TC practices to view the outside social environment as relatively stable and acceptable, and patients' behaviour in relation to it as problematic. This thereby opened up a possible awareness and critique of social structures and power relations. This movement emphasised the importance of revealing and throwing into relief contradictions inherent in the institution, and sent out a powerful cautionary note to overzealous therapy that does not attend to wider social conflicts (Donnelly 1992). Furthermore, Basaglia criticised the absence of an ongoing focus on change, innovation and dialectical thinking in British anti-psychiatry, as well as more generally in TCs. In arguing for a rethinking of the relationship between TCs and wider social movements I will later draw on Basaglia's (1987) proposal that the TC should be viewed and developed as a transitional space rather than an end in itself.

## Therapeutic communities and the user movement

In this historical context it is perhaps not surprising to note a convergence between TCs and the emerging patients/service user movement. However, recent attempts to explore this have only resulted in an exposition of *indirect* links, specifically forged through connections between TCs and anti-psychiatry rather than any direct links with TCs (Coppock and Hopton 2000; Tucker 2001). Coppock and Hopton argue that there is an indirect link between the service user movement and the history of the TCs through the inspiration and critique that 'anti-psychiatry' provided to the emerging patients' move-ment in the late 1960s and early 1970s. Similarly, Tucker (2001) argues that there is a historical convergence between TC practice and the service user movement, particularly through TCs' work with psychosis via the work of Laing and colleagues at Kingsley Hall that fed into and inspired both the pa-tients' movement and TCs. Perhaps overstating the case, Tucker suggests that the contemporary user movement was historically motivated through ideas pioneered in the TC field (Tucker 2001, p.240).

At the same time TCs have been criticised for their lack of genuine at-tempts at democratisation and their sparse attention to the reality of the wider social context in which they operate. Indeed, there have been few serious at-tempts at evaluating TCs on the basis of service user involvement or empower-ment. Notable exceptions include two useful articles on the process and exam-ples of good practice around democratisation (Crozier 1979; Winship 1997).

It is often assumed that 'user involvement' is at the heart of TC practice and that, by definition, TCs 'must be' empowering (Allen 1992, p.254). Yet these assumptions all too readily equate empowerment with therapy (see Barnes and Bowl 2001). The conflation of such terms in practice serves only to de-politicise both, and renders empowerment, as a specific political process in itself, superfluous. Furthermore, recent concerns have been expressed about the gap between the ideals of TC collective practice, and the reality of its current limitations in terms of, for example, empowerment and participation (Hopton 2000; Manning 1989; Winship 1995, 1997).

There have been various critiques of therapeutic communities, the most important of which has focused upon the role of TCs in imposing social control, regulation and surveillance (Bloor and McIntosh 1990; Perrow 1965; Sharp 1975; Sugarman 1975). These critiques questioned the group norms and standards to which individuals are supposed to conform. Service users' views of TCs have often echoed this critique, particularly the way TCs use patients themselves as the primary agents of exerting peer control. Patients in TCs have referred to this process as patients becoming 'little staff' (Sharp 1975) or the 'equivalent of the chief of police' (Mahony 1979, p.81). Indeed, it has been noted that most patient resistance in TCs is against surveillance (Bloor *et al.* 1988).

> It is very difficult to maintain one's integrity under the therapeutic commu-nity system. Patients are required – in plain English – to rat on one another. Resisting the system can result in punishment. Patients are required to

enforce the standards and expectations of the staff. (Chamberlain 1988, p.17)

The idea that TCs could be radical alternatives to traditional psychiatry can be viewed either as reappraising the innovative potential of TCs, or alternatively as developments merely at the 'softer' end of psychiatry. Brandon (1991) argued that although TCs were better than enforced incarceration, there is nothing intrinsically 'alternative' or 'radical' about TC practice, as it is dependent on the dominant psychiatric treatment against which our expectations of alternatives are measured. Similarly, Hopton points out that during the 1970s service users were more marginalised, so the TC approach was the only example of user-centred practice to make a significant impact on mainstream mental health care (Hopton 2000). Viewed in this way it is not surprising that both anti-psychiatry and the patient/user movement had connections with TCs. However, once the radical political climate and the counter-cultural movements receded, unless the TC movement sustained its innovation and critique by being nourished by more modern counter-cultural forces, it was liable to be left behind.

In the meantime, the situation has evolved, not least because of rising expectations and emerging demands from the service user movement. Ongoing challenges to psychiatric power and knowledge (O'Hagan 1993) have led to the development of a proliferation of alternatives such as user-led practices (Lindow 1994) and initiatives developed around the notion of 'post-psychiatry' and critical psychiatry, which have moved beyond the development of specific alternative services (Bracken and Thomas 2005).

Through the construction of an alternative history and analysis, this book examines the limitations and possibilities of therapeutic communities as radical initiatives in mental health services. It raises ongoing difficult questions about the development of alternative mental health practices. Equally, it explores the connections between the user movement, therapeutic communities, critiques of psychiatry and psychoanalytic models of intervention. So we will now turn to the place of Paddington Day Hospital as one key site in that history.

## Paddington Day Hospital: a site of convergence

The anti-psychiatry movement, the TC movement and the emerging patients' movement converged for a time around Paddington Day Hospital. One of the founder members of the Mental Patient's Union illustrates the importance of Paddington in the history of the emerging radical mental health movements:

> Paddington Day Hospital provided the sort of, the backdrop effectively to what was a very political awareness about the way in which patients were being treated... It just made an awful lot of sense really that the issues around mental health and the issues around individuals struggling for rights fit somewhere within that political context... I think unless there had been a Paddington Day Hospital, those issues I don't think would have really come to the fore. You had lots of little groups or strands here, there and everywhere, but the Paddington Day Hospital was like a focus for everybody. (Douieb 2000)

In the early 1970s, Paddington functioned as a materialised, visible and symbolic 'space of convergence' of various counter-cultural forces. It was an important point of connection and communication in the UK radical (anti-) psychiatric community. This specific, local convergent site resulted in a rich process of fermentation, crystallising many existing progressive tendencies:

> A convergent space implies a heterogeneous affinity of common ground between various social movements, grass roots initiatives, non-governmental organisations and other formations, wherein certain interests, goals, tactics and strategies converge. It is a space of facilitation, solidarity, communication, co-ordination and information sharing. (Routledge 2001, p.1)

The idea of a 'convergent space' helps us to understand how such periods of social conflict can bring together such a rich mixture of previously disparate groups and individuals. Through a collective understanding of their ideas and experiences they are able to shape new forms of dialogue and action. Paddington became a rallying point for criticism of mainstream psychiatry. It occupied a critical space in the conceptualisation and provision of alternatives to psychiatry while it was being developed as part of a more radical, libertarian and permissive approach to TCs. The conceptualisations of 'working utopias' are important in the history of radical mental health movements (Crossley 1999b). Working utopias are concrete mini-realisations of imagined changes desired by the movement. They are 'working sites' of alternative practices or 'laboratories of experience' that bring together radical practitioners, activists and theorists, providing common reference points as well as actual meeting places for the ongoing generation of radical ideas (Crossley 1999b, p.827). They are important in reproducing social movement ideas and activism. Crossley argued that Kingsley Hall and Trieste (where many aspects of the Italian democratic psychiatry movement were realised) served important symbolic and material functions in post-war British radical mental health movements.

Paddington was not a working utopia in any sustained sense. However, in the early 1970s it was able to boost the imaginative force of practitioners, patients and activists. It provided them with the possibility of envisioning the creation of alternatives and the impetus to continue and develop radical ideas and organisations. Innovative skills and dispositions are more likely to develop in new and unusual situations, which can prompt and consolidate these changes. The practices at Paddington generated alternative understandings and practices and it functioned as an important meeting place for a number of new groups and organisations as well as being regularly visited by local and international visitors keen to develop similar practices.

Paddington was also to function as an important site of innovation, conflict and debate within the theory and practice of therapeutic communities in the UK. At its best, Paddington was a thriving, exciting, outward-looking therapeutic community. Paddington was frequently mentioned and referred to in the early TC literature, perhaps suggesting its centrality the TC movement at the time. Often seen as something to aspire to, it was also, at the very least, viewed as being seen part of the 'range' of TC practice. Paddington was seen to occupy the 'radical' end of the spectrum from the more established TCs such as the Henderson Hospital (Hinshelwood and Grunberg 1979). To some degree the ideas of permissiveness, informality, egalitarianism and social action were being explored more generally in TCs at that time. For example, when the Association of Therapeutic Communities (ATC) was formed in the early 1970s, numerous debates raged concerning the contradictions between TCs and the wider social environment, the conflict between individual adjustment and social change, and the importance of understanding social reality and of resisting authoritarian structures and institutions. However, Paddington tested out and explored some of these wider issues to a greater extent and this resulted in social action through and beyond the TC itself.

Although it is not as well known as many other TCs, Paddington has entered therapeutic community and mental health folklore through its vivid portrayal in Claire Baron's *Asylum to Anarchy* (Baron 1987). This was the most comprehensive published work on Paddington and still remains the dominant account. Baron portrayed Paddington as a radical experiment in mental health democracy and liberty, which descended into anarchy, chaos and tyranny. By 1979, after patients' complaints and two official inquiries into its functioning, the consultant, Julian Goodburn, was sacked and the day hospital closed.

Readers of *Asylum to Anarchy* are often unaware of the identity of the day hospital featured in Baron's book; for example, Clarke recently mistakenly referred to it as Marlborough Day Hospital (Clarke 2004). Despite this, it has become a well-known and highly referenced source, particularly in the history of therapeutic communities, but also in mental health services generally. It is often used as a cautionary tale, both of the unrestrained use of psychoanalytic interpretation within therapeutic communities, and the dangers of libertarianism, democratisation and radicalism within mental health practices. Baron's persuasive but one-sided narrative about Paddington presented digestible conclusions and assumptions to its readers and subsequently has influenced the direction of TCs as well as permeating the consciousness of therapeutic community practitioners.

However, the fuller history of Paddington Day Hospital is less well known. The successful campaign to defend it from closure in 1971/2, and the subsequent development of the Mental Patients Union (MPU) in 1973, were important events in the formation of the mental health service user movement. The MPU is considered to be the first overtly politicised patients' group in the UK (Crossley 1999a; Durkin and Douieb 1975; Van de Graaf 1989a, b) and is regarded as a 'defining moment in the history of mental health' (Crossley 1999a, p.668).

However, while there have been numerous commentaries about Paddington in the therapeutic community literature, they almost exclusively focus on the later crisis at Paddington. For example, the MPU has rarely figured in any of these accounts and is mentioned only briefly in *Asylum to Anarchy* (Baron 1987). On the other hand, while Paddington was highlighted in an analysis of the history of the patients' movement, this was viewed in isolation from consideration of the subsequent plight of Paddington (Crossley 1999a). In other words, commentators on Paddington have overlooked discussions of the benefits and possibilities of the protest and MPU, while commentators on MPU and the patients' movement have ignored the more complex issues that these struggles highlighted. The complexities that arose at Paddington – difficulties vividly portrayed in Baron's book – make the understanding of its history and development important and necessary.

In the following chapters in this book I will examine how Paddington served as a pioneering example of innovative practice in the history of therapeutic communities and the patients' movement and yet was subsequently widely viewed as an example of bad therapeutic practice. This book attempts to understand how Paddington moved from being so strongly fought for, to being vilified and condemned. While demanding critical re-appraisal, these events resist easy interpretation. This retrospective research into Paddington, unlike official inquiries or commentaries immediately after its demise, is not tied down to immediate legal or professional concerns such as deciding upon its worth, harm or ultimate fate. Rather, it attempts to re-open certain areas of interest and debate that have been prematurely closed off.

My aim is to question the implicitly normalising and dominant accounts that have produced Paddington as an aberration. I do not necessarily view Paddington as a model of 'good practice' – and, indeed, it is not possible to produce any real 'evidence' either way without being able to follow up significant numbers of ex-patients, which was not possible. However, I argue for a re-appraisal of some of the questions Paddington raised and the ideas it promoted. Moreover, some of the issues that it grappled with in the 1970s were not so far removed from many of our current concerns in the field of mental health. Paddington highlighted fundamental difficulties in the application of psychoanalytic theory within TCs; however, the tendency to scapegoat Paddington meant that these more general lessons have been lost.

The analysis presented here informs an exploration of wider questions regarding the importance of social movements and critical social theory in therapeutic communities and the need for continued innovation and experimentation. By interrogating the history and interpretations of Paddington Day Hospital, I aim to recapture the radicalism and aspirations, as well as the conflicts and difficulties, of the therapeutic community movement. I believe these issues need extensive consideration and discussion before it will be possible to develop more democratic mental health services and pursue a radical therapeutic community agenda.

## Asylum to Action

In Chapter Two I aim to give a brief flavour of the Paddington Day Hospital in its early years and review some of the more progressive ideas that influenced its development. Chapter Three describes the 'Victorious Protest' at Paddington in 1971 which saved it from unwanted transfer to a more traditional hospital setting and possible closure. I explore the wider context in which these protests took place and consider the developing practices at the day hospital that helped provide the impetus and solidarity on which the protests were dependent. It highlights connections between therapeutic community practices and the possibilities and limitations of patients' social action. These protests brought together previously disparate strands of anti-psychiatry sentiment alongside other emerging resistance both within and beyond psychiatry and helped kick-start a national patients' movement.

Chapter Four draws out links between the development of the Mental Patients Union (MPU) and Paddington Day Hospital, specifically exploring some of the emerging tensions and conflicts in its formation and development. I outline the development of the MPU as a separate organisation and examine its enduring effects on the history and consciousness of a growing mental health movement.

The shared vision developed between patients and staff at Paddington Day Hospital was to become strained when differences arose between patients' demands and the particular analytic psychotherapeutic approach that was increasingly insisted upon by the staff. Chapter Five attempts to understand the approach that evolved at the day hospital after the protests and action, and explores the particular manifestations of the tensions and conflicts that this created.

Having provided an alternative narrative of Paddington, subsequent chapters examine the limitations of dominant theoretical models and practice-based reactions that have been used to understand, explain and respond to the crisis at Paddington. Chapters Six and Seven specifically challenge dominant accounts of Paddington in order to open up different possibilities for analysis and understanding. First, Chapter Six explores the usefulness and limitations of Claire Baron's *Asylum to Anarchy* and Bob Hobson's influential theory of the 'Messianic Community' (Hobson 1979). Chapter Seven then examines how dominant accounts function as a 'culturally available narrative', reinforcing stories of radical failure. It goes on to describe the way in which Paddington was pathologised, and then considers how notions of medical and psychiatric 'acceptability' were mobilised in responses to the fate of Paddington.

Moving on from historical accounts, Chapter Eight draws upon an additional piece of research into a contemporary day-unit therapeutic community. It uses this analysis to ascertain whether modern TC practices have in fact moved from 'Anarchy' to 'Asylum'. In other words, it looks at whether the turn away from the more libertarian TCs such as Paddington and the institution of an increasingly structured and regulated environment in modern TCs have adequately addressed the difficulties encountered at Paddington. I argue that, on the contrary, these difficulties highlighted crucial dilemmas that were not just specific to Paddington, but are in fact ongoing dilemmas in current therapeutic community practices. In part, this is because of the continued predominance of psychoanalysis as the privileged framework of understanding in TCs at the expense of the development of more collective formulations. Such formulations might, for example, relate to notions of group solidarity and collective identity.

TCs will always evolve in response to their wider social and historical context. By its very nature, that context is continually shifting, and particular opportunities for innovation are often created at specific historical moments.

The concluding chapter addresses this historic specificity. It outlines some of the more significant changes in the mental health field that have occurred since Paddington and how these might open up, or close down, opportunities for TCs to contribute to this process of deepening democracy and self-determination.

# CHAPTER TWO

# Paddington Day Hospital
## The Early Years

Paddington Day Hospital existed, in one form or another, for 17 years (1962–1979). It was to become one of the first non-residential therapeutic communities in Britain and a founding member of the Association of Therapeutic Communities in 1972. This chapter describes the history of Paddington and gives a flavour of its rich and contradictory development through some examples, quotes and illustrations. It reviews some of the theoretical and cultural influences on the more progressive elements of the day hospital – thus setting the context for the following three chapters, which re-construct some of the key events during its existence.

Structurally, the day hospital was part of the building that housed the Paddington Clinic and Day Hospital, alongside an adult out-patients department and a Child Guidance Clinic. This whole organisation was later renamed the Paddington Centre for Psychotherapy. The main contribution of the centre as a whole was its use of psychoanalytic psychotherapies (Hall 1979). Indeed, the centre was attempting to gain a firm psychoanalytic foothold in the National Health Service (NHS) and it was recognised as the first psychoanalytic clinic within the NHS in England. There were plans to set up a training institute for psychodynamic studies within the centre but this idea was later scrapped, in part many believed because of the negative publicity caused by later events at the day hospital.

While it is clear that psychoanalytic theory played an increasingly major part in the development of Paddington, its practice changed and developed over time and so to identify one theoretical approach as central to its development would belie the complexity of that development. Therefore, it is important to understand the multiple influences that came to bear on the day hospital and to understand how its practice emerged and developed from a complex theoretical and social context.

The day hospital was initially set up in 1962 as a conventional out-patient rehabilitation facility. Its early function was to aid the return of patients to the community from Horton Hospital in Epsom, Surrey. The therapeutic milieu in the early 1960s was based on traditional, medicalised day hospital procedures. Short stay was encouraged, and it included physical treatments like ECT and drugs, as well as behaviour therapy and occupational therapy (Goodburn 1986; Gregory 1968; Hall 1979).

Although the day hospital had some degree of autonomy it was answerable to the medical committee of the centre that oversaw its development. As the day hospital increasingly questioned conventional attitudes towards treatment during the 1960s, it was reported that the adult outpatients department continued to use ECT, drug therapy, behaviour therapy and even splints for limp penises (Goodburn 1986). In the early 1960s, the consultant Basil Gregory, tried to introduce a more group-based therapeutic approach into the day hospital. Initially, many staff resisted this change until a number of new appointments were made involving, most notably, key staff who had worked at the Henderson Hospital therapeutic community in Surrey. From the mid-1960s, the day hospital was developed in line with concepts of a 'therapeutic community' based on an increasingly group-based treatment programme and a shared decision-making philosophy that revolved around patient participation in the actual community process as the main therapeutic agent. By 1968, the day hospital had an established reputation as a TC (Crocket 1978). The community processes consisted of small psychotherapy groups, large community meetings, daily work groups and admission and assessment meetings involving staff and patients. In addition, on patients' request they were able to attend some of the formal staff meetings, which was seen as being important to facilitate genuine staff/patient participation (Gregory 1968).

This approach was gradually promoted by staff at the day hospital and strong links were built with the outside community. This developed over a number of years but there was a lull in the late 1960s when patient numbers dropped, admission criteria became stricter and the rules and sanctions operating within the community became more rigid (Hall 1979). The 'democratic' aspirations of the staff and the day hospital were increasingly put to the test. Gregory gradually became disillusioned with the more democratising elements of the TC approach, and thought that patients were beginning to take over what should be medical decisions. This seemed to culminate when patients wanted to try and support a patient who was experiencing 'psychosis' in the community. Gregory used his 'latent' authority to veto the community's decision as he felt the patient should go into hospital, and over-ruled the democratic will of the patients (Hall 1979; Lemlij et al. 1979).

Shortly after, Gregory left to become the medical director of Horton Hospital in 1970. Despite his disillusionment, he recommended that he be replaced by his former understudy Julian Goodburn, who had worked with Gregory at Paddington from 1964–1966. Goodburn was an up-and-coming young psychiatrist and psychoanalyst who had worked and studied psychoanalysis at the Tavistock Clinic and was keen to explore the use of psychoanalysis, patient involvement and democratising processes within a TC context. Goodburn was destined to embody, represent and re-create the aspirations and disappointments of radical psychiatrists. He became notorious in the therapeutic community field through his involvement in Paddington and indirectly via two anonymised depictions in Claire Baron's *Asylum to Anarchy* (Baron 1987) and Erica Jong's fictional narrative *Fear of Flying* (Jong 1974). Jong's depiction of a young Laingian analyst 'Adrian Goodlove' signified the disappointment and the false hopes represented by individual men and radical psychotherapists. The speculation that Jong's protagonist was actually based on Goodburn resurfaced in Baron's account of Goodburn, whom she called 'Adrian' in *Asylum to Anarchy*.

Goodburn returned to Paddington as a locum, and, with the other members of staff, began to develop an increasingly informal and egalitarian environment, expanding its openness and democratic zeal and injecting a more libertarian atmosphere as well as more traditionally psychoanalytic ideas into its frame. It was felt that the community should be able to tolerate a greater level of distress and a wider variety of patients were admitted, including those who had experienced 'psychosis', and the 'mixture of patients seemed to work well' (Hall 1979, p.4). At this time TCs were more willing to work therapeutically with people diagnosed with 'psychosis' and, in this spirit, Paddington was a serious attempt at a non-medicalised alternative to hospitalisation. It also responded to patients' demands for an environment in which they could support each other through a severe mental health crisis.

Under Gregory, the day hospital had looked towards adopting a more standard and structured therapeutic community approach modelled on the Henderson Hospital. Yet, Goodburn and his colleagues were unhappy with this model and thought it too rigid and authoritarian. Rules were relaxed and Paddington took on a 'new lease of life' (Hall 1979, p.4). Their critique viewed more conventional TCs like the Henderson as inviting and encouraging inauthentic 'false self' responses in relation to the wider standards of society. Through harassing patients to conform to their institutional demands, these conventional TCs were seen as imposing a harsh group superego similar to that which was likely to have contributed to people's problems and symptoms in the first place (Goodburn 1976). Without a challenge to, and possible modification of, these wider societal expectations within the TC's own rules and regulations, little real change was possible or desirable.

Similar ideas had also inspired the likes of R.D. Laing, David Cooper and Loren Mosher to set up alternative and more libertarian therapeutic communities such as Kingsley Hall, Villa 21 and Soteria House respectively. The notion of a 'false self' developing in relation to norms and values that were transmitted and reproduced from society via the family and psychiatry was popularised through R.D. Laing's *The Divided Self* (1960). In this, Laing had added a more radicalised and existential angle to some of the ideas of D.W. Winnicott (Burston 1996). These ideas also coincided with a growing counter-cultural utilisation of the ideas of other radical psychoanalysts such as Wilhelm Reich. Reich had suggested that opposition to authoritarian forces and bourgeois moralities could reduce mental distress (Reich 1975). All these approaches had in common a profoundly ambitious and positive risk-taking approach, which believed that recovery was possible in the development of an alternative, accepting context that challenged conventional structures of hierarchies and notions of normality.

We can see these ideas at work in Paddington, which attempted to limit the perceived power of institutions over individuals. The day hospital increasingly tried to enable patients to develop their own structures rather than imposing a group (or societal) norm on patients' behaviours. Thus a key idea that influenced Paddington was that patients should be left to organise their own lives without too much aid or interference from staff (Crocket 1978).

Anyone coming to the Paddington at this time would have been treated to a relaxed, *laissez-faire* atmosphere. Both staff and patients would take part in lengthy discussions about a variety of personal, social and political issues. As one participant recalled:

> There was an awful lot of talk going on, and then suddenly somebody would think of something new... We used to sit around for hours listening to Leonard Cohen and Cyril Kingham... [Cohen's] 'Like a Bird on the Wire', that was the one that was just non-stop. (Douieb 2000)

This participant recalled how the culture was challenging and yet was supportive, experimental and also affirming. It united people who came together with a variety of presenting problems, conflicts and diagnoses such as schizophrenia, obsessions, depression, phobias and character disorders. Cohen's lyrics 'like a bird on the wire, like a drunk in a midnight choir, I have tried in my way to be free' (Cohen 1969) set the scene for what at times was a united desire to find more liberatory ways to rid themselves of their afflictions, both internal(ised) and imposed, and to seek personal and political transformation.

We can see that within the day hospital an emphasis was placed on resisting the pressure of social expectations. Patients and staff were interested in examining the relationship or disjunction between their own values and feelings and those to which they were expected to conform. As one of the staff commented, 'Such an approach leads to a growth in self-awareness, [and] a maximisation of the power each individual has in society' (Durkin 1972a, p.14). Paddington did not focus on rehabilitation in the sense of returning the individual to the family or production line, but rather encouraged each person to realise his or her full potential in whatever way possible and however long it took.

There is little written reference in the Paddington literature to the influence of 'anti-psychiatry' theorists as such, yet it was identified as implicit in the culture of the day hospital (Baron 1984a, 1987; Crossley 1999a; Durkin 1972a). For example, Baron highlighted the influence of anti-psychiatry in conversations in the day hospital where, she argued, both 'staff and patients largely subscribe to the anti-psychiatry ideology which argues that madness is but sanity in an insane world' (1984a, p.247).

That the individual patient is a 'bearer' of wider social contradictions was an important thread in the literature of R.D. Laing and David Cooper and was very much part of the culture of the day hospital. Durkin (1972a) specifically drew attention to how Paddington challenged the way individuals are elected and scapegoated by society into being ill in order for that society to avoid dealing with the madness of wider social settings and institutions. Goodburn expressed this idea again when I interviewed him for this research:

> How does one understand the transformations and the representations of the external situation in the dynamics of the one which is under immediate study?... Somewhere or other there is a correlation between the contradiction, or disquiet that they're experiencing, and the contradiction or disquiet that everybody ought to be experiencing *à propos* some factor of society at large, which...they are, through circumstances of their particular experience, the bearer of – the victim of, you might even say. [They] will subsequently manifest this as if it were something solely going on in them, when in fact, it is going on in them...as a consequence of the fact that these issues are not resolved in the world at large... It just happens that they are the person standing on that particular street corner at that particular time who has copped it, as it were. (Goodburn 2000)

Some took such ideas further and argued that Paddington was 'an essential challenge to the traditional role expected of a psychiatric institution' (Durkin

1972a, p.13). In this way, the aim of the day hospital was to investigate the dialectical relationship between individuals and their social situation:

> In group psychotherapy at Paddington emotions are analysed in relation to the total ongoing social situation. For example, the distinction between staff and patients is maintained because it is a reality. However, this power structure is continually questioned. Why are the staff paid salaries while the patients have to survive on social security? This in itself reflects a status difference which is examined in relation to the social structure external to the hospital. (p.14)

We can see that part of the understanding at Paddington was to challenge the social expectations of a mental patient status that effectively disenfranchised the person and led to them remaining powerless, lacking in agency and renouncing responsibility for their lives and social change.

> He [Goodburn] used to say, you know, 'All these processes have led to you coming here, being in this role, but I'm not going to perpetuate it. I'm not going to be part of the system that put you here, you know.' (Davies 2000)

Paddington tried a range of creative, challenging and often unorthodox means to readdress this passivity and patients' internalisation of their medicalisation. Evidently articulate and charismatic, Goodburn especially had a confrontational therapy style, pushing issues to their limits in an attempt to force change. For example, one participant recalled how, on one occasion, Goodburn sat under a table refusing to make decisions of behalf of the patients, forcing them to take responsibility for their own lives and actions (Davies 2000). This view of the need for patient responsibility continued at Paddington throughout the 1970s and was one that Goodburn particularly stressed. For example in an interview in the local paper, he was quoted as saying 'the patient who classifies himself as a patient no longer has to think about his life' (Paddington Mercury 1976a, p.1).

More specifically, patients were encouraged to understand their need to be designated 'mentally ill'. As far as possible, prescribing medication and other palliatives was avoided as this was seen to be at odds with the therapeutic approach. When some patients who were increasingly desperate for solutions and relief asked for pills and advice:

> [Goodburn's] standard phrase was 'I'm not going to be your policeman. If you want an external solution to your problems, I can, you know, put you in touch with someone who will give you a pill, and [you can] take something

external and put it into your body, and that's the control coming from outside. And if that's what you want, go away and do it somewhere else. But I'm not going to be doing that with you here.' And so all the change had to come from within the person...and that was the principle of it. (Davies 2000)

Paddington attempted to work with patients who would not normally be accepted into NHS psychotherapy services because they were considered as 'unsuitable' or 'too sick' for such interventions. Goodburn argued that out-patient psychotherapy or group analysis was often only accessible to particular patients whose disturbance was relatively contained and was restricted to those who continued to live and work in the wider community. Partly because of this another principle that became enshrined in the day hospital was that patients could attend the day hospital for as long as they wanted to and referrals were not restricted to a particular catchment area. Thus while officially the length of stay was deemed to be two years and entry restricted to patients attending from a specific catchment area, in reality some patients attended for longer and came from further afield.

Gradually, an open admission procedure was developed, whereby the traditional TC approach of a group discussion and decision before admission was gradually replaced by more informal and self-determined access. Attendance at Paddington was voluntary, and increasingly people came by self-referrals (often via word of mouth) and there were no waiting lists. To some extent Paddington managed to operate such that even during its highest attendance rate, patients would self-regulate their own attendance so there were never too many patients attending at any one time (Goodburn 1976; Reder 1976).

Paddington tried not to give out diagnoses, and insisted that other medical conventions such as ensuring the presence of designated clinicians at all times were unnecessary. Administrative and bureaucratic procedures such as case notes and record keeping were all kept to a minimum. In addition, as a result of not wanting to perpetuate people's role as helpless victims and 'mental patients', staff often queried the need to sign patients' medical certificates because they wanted to challenge their need to be designated 'sick'. Many of these ideas at Paddington conflicted with other professionals in the centre and the wider psychiatric and medical community who demanded diagnoses, assessments or assessments of 'risk'. Tensions and rifts began to appear between the day hospital and the surrounding psychiatric services. More widely, we can see how this became increasingly problematic in a structured and regulated statutory NHS context that demands specific criteria for funding, referrals and the provision of time-limited services for particular medically defined categories of patients.

The idea that patients should not be 'singled out' as pathological often resulted in other, more outward-looking social initiatives and opportunities beyond the confines of the day hospital. Indeed, during this time it was felt that the day hospital had made involvement with the local community an integral part of its functioning (Durkin 1972a, b). Such initiatives included providing evening opportunities for patients and their families to explore their situation, groups for 'struggling housewives' and regular seminars held for GPs and other local workers. In addition, patients and staff developed various activities in the local community, for example an afternoon group for local residents who had few social contacts, and a market stall set up on the Portobello Road run by patients.

More significantly, patients were involved in setting up a patient's commune. The idea of finding alternative accommodation had been discussed for some time in the day hospital as many patients lived in inadequate and/or temporary accommodation or with their families/parents. Eventually, patients and staff agreed to set up alternative local accommodation connected to Paddington, the Fordingly commune (Hall 1973). This included temporary beds for emergency accommodation, which was managed by a team including residents, staff and housing trust representatives.

The senior occupational therapist at Paddington, Mary Hall, documented the development of the commune at the time (Hall 1972, 1973). She explained how an agreement was made that residents would attempt to work out any living difficulties with each other and only bring them into the day hospital when they couldn't. After some initial difficulties, she described how the commune was able to manage its own affairs without any serious problems:

> All residents now seem to be more mature and able people, having some confidence that that they can cope with their own problems or be able to solve them on their own. The need for some authority figure of guardian seems to have evaporated. For many the realisation that they had abilities to create something worthwhile was a positive part of their treatment. (1972, p.2814)

Such initiatives were seen as a positive part of treatment, challenging patients' isolation, developing social networks and testing out their ability to do something collectively that many patients found frightening or disturbing. At this time the necessity of developing a social action perspective alongside the development of psychoanalytic ideas in the day hospital was seen to be crucial. Goodburn made this link explicit:

> Psychoanalytic principles form the background, but are modified in relation to this unique situation where all concerned can not only explore their inner worlds, and check their findings by interaction with others (as in out-patient group psychotherapy) but also take social action where appropriate, for example patients dissatisfied with inadequate housing – digs, hostels – raised money, rented a house, and now manage their own affairs in this respect. (1972, p.459)

With its mixed programme of regular therapy groups, community meetings and use of psychoanalysis, its flexible approach to group therapeutic boundaries and structures and its participation in wider social networks and activities, Paddington was a hybrid between a traditional TC and a more radical and libertarian TC. Yet its increasing adherence to psychoanalysis as its primary theoretical framework was to set it apart from other 'anti-psychiatric' TC initiatives – and this psychoanalytic influence, paradoxically, brought it closer to more mainstream TCs.

There were numerous tensions evident in the practice at Paddington. For example, there was a conflict between the idea of challenging patients' assumed patient status and then actually providing a designated service particularly 'for' people deemed too 'ill' for conventional therapeutic intervention. Another tension existed between the wish to promote patient autonomy and the potential for this to be used to undermine the very philosophy on which its practice was based. A further tension related to promoting collective and non-hierarchical forms of self-organisation while adhering to theories of unconscious motivation that only trained psychoanalytical 'experts' could understand and reveal. These tensions ran right through the history of Paddington. These tensions are crucial, not only because they continue to figure in TCs generally, but also because they relate to various tensions involved in political action in mental health services generally. This, in turn, impacts on the potential for meaningful dialogue and solidarity between patients, service users and professionals.

While the approach adopted at Paddington often proved fruitful, these tensions frequently created resistance and challenge from patients – for example, when staff challenged the need to sign medical certificates. Although patients needed medical certificates in order to claim social security benefits, Goodburn thought they should get it signed elsewhere as it would interfere with the particular therapeutic approach he was developing. Yet to get them signed elsewhere still required another designated medical professional to declare that the patient was ill and this epitomised a wider contradiction that was hard to solve in the context of the day hospital.

Brian Haddon, a nurse at Paddington, documented an example that occurred in the summer of 1971 some months before the threat of transfer and subsequent protest that is explored in the next chapter. Haddon (1979) recalled an instance when staff were unable to find Goodburn after one of the small therapy groups run at the day hospital, and thought the group must have over-run. Shortly after, they found him barricaded in one of the rooms by a group of patients who would not let him out until he agreed to sign their medical certificates. At this time, the situation was relatively contained and a compromise was reached. However, following instances like this some patients refused to return and took sanctuary elsewhere, away from what they considered to be 'ego-tripping existential psychiatrists' (Small, undated). This was an example of the initial skirmishes in the battle that was to develop at Paddington.

Despite the ongoing struggles and tensions Paddington was flourishing and had approximately 50 registered patients (Hall 1979). It was seen by many as being a pioneer within the TC movement and, to some degree, was an inspiration to other TCs. During this time Paddington became a sought-after place of work and many staff felt they were at the 'cutting edge' of radical new developments and ideas.

However, in the midst of these developments and innovations, rumours suggested that the day hospital would be transferred and ultimately closed. Patients and staff united to oppose this move. Although Paddington was by no means perfect, it offered a chance of something different. A young social work student, Liz Durkin, was on placement at the clinic upstairs. She was so inspired by the day hospital that she increasingly spent most of her time there. When the threat arose she agreed to co-ordinate the campaign. She was later to become one of the main activists in setting up the Mental Patients' Union alongside Eric Irwin, a long-standing patient in the day hospital, political activist, Marxist and big inspiration to the emerging patients' movement (Curtis *et al.* 2000; Van de Graaf 1989a, b).

This was the perfect opportunity for the expression and articulation of an emerging critique of psychiatry and the politics of mental health. These ideas also seemed to resonate with some of the strategies being developed at Paddington itself. Perhaps the tactics employed by the Goodburn and his team were paying off. The patients were not going to be passive victims and see their community taken over: they would fight for it. The following chapter explores the ways in which some of the ideas at Paddington were developed and expanded upon during the campaign.

# CHAPTER THREE

# Protest and Social Action

This chapter explores the events during 1971–1972 at Paddington Day Hospital in what was dubbed the 'Victorious Protest' that saved the day hospital from unwanted transfer to a more 'traditional' acute psychiatry service and possible closure (Hall 1979; Ward 1972). The latent potential for resistance had been brewing in and against psychiatry for some time and this became articulated through collective action to defend the day hospital. The protests highlighted connections between therapeutic community practices and the possibilities of patients' challenge and social action within, in defence of and beyond a therapeutic community. This chapter describes these events and reviews some of the debates and issues that emerged during the campaign. It then considers the particular practices at Paddington that helped to develop the impetus and solidarity on which the protests were dependent. Finally, it explores the importance of the wider context within which the protests took place.

## The 'victorious protest'

The protests were a response to a proposal for St Mary's District Psychiatric Service to take over facilities provided by the Paddington Centre. At first it seemed the whole centre was under threat but it soon became clear that the day hospital was to be most affected and that day hospital patients would effectively be transferred to St Mary's. This was perceived as a threat to the practices at the day hospital by both patients and staff for several reasons. It was clearly stated that St Mary's was unable, within existing resources, to run the day hospital as a therapeutic community and that it would be run on 'different lines'. It was reported that St Mary's was well known to emphasise more physical and bio-chemical methods of treatment (Benn 1972). In addition, it seemed that treatment would primarily be short term, since in the newly established District General Hospitals the average length of stay was reported to be three weeks. In addition, participants were worried that this might reduce the opportunity for innovation and radical initiatives.

The proposed change typified an emerging national policy trend to reorganise psychiatric services by incorporating psychiatric units into district general hospitals. One of the main reasons given for this particular transfer was 'administrative efficiency' (although the campaign highlighted how this was, in fact, connected with wider issues of economics and psychiatric ideology). Other therapeutic communities were also threatened by hospital authorities during this time – for example, Marlborough Day Hospital (Paddington's neighbour) and Halliwick Hospital (Haddon 1979). Paradoxically this was a time often seen as the therapeutic community movement's 'golden age', reflected by the Royal College of Psychiatrists' recommendation that training in psychiatry should involve experience in therapeutic communities (Benn 1972, p.45). Despite this, Durkin (1972a, b) noted that not all TCs in the country wholeheartedly backed the protest.

For a variety of reasons it was agreed in the medical committee of the Paddington Centre to oppose the take-over plan. An action group was formed out of an interdisciplinary community group that was already in existence and had been initiated at the day hospital for community workers, social workers, GPs, nurses and patients. This group had been meeting regularly to discuss wider issues of interest in the community and run seminars. Staff and patients formed an action committee and contacted the media, MPs, GPs and other mental health groups and political organisations. These links helped the protest gain momentum and it attracted local and national press coverage. Local newspapers took a keen interest and it was also covered in many professional journals such as *World Medicine* (Benn 1972), *Social Work Today* (Durkin 1972a; Smith 1972) and the *Nursing Times* (Kavalier 1972). The protests were highlighted in the radical and alternative press, especially in the emerging radical psychology and anti-psychiatry literature as well in some of the socialist and anarchist press.

During this time Paddington inspired a great deal of loyalty amongst patients, staff and other organisations. Participants were determined that the radical and democratising elements that had been developed in the therapeutic community would not be lost. The joint staff/patient action group stated that if they did not save Paddington, they would consider other ways of continuing their work. The campaign was well supported by a variety of organisations, including the National Association for Mental Health (now MIND) and the Patients Association, and 6000 people signed a petition to the Secretary of State – a petition that included the signatures of 22 MPs. A large public meeting was organised by the action group in March 1972 and the local paper reported that 900 people attended (Paddington Mercury 1972, p.1). The importance of outside support in sustaining a long protest has been noted in more recent struggles to save therapeutic communities from closure (Robinson 1994).

In the meantime many patients wrote letters in support of the day hospital. One explained how his mental health had improved after sixteen months at Paddington, having previously been treated with drugs and ECT:

> Having experienced one of the alternatives to group therapy, namely the taking of drugs, I do not believe they could have helped me the way the group therapy has. Because of this I would like to see the retention of the Paddington Day Clinic and other communities based on the same structure. I am against the present policy of the NHS, which is to phase this form of treatment out and replace it with hospitals operating on a quick turnover of patients. Patients would then be prescribed with drugs to relieve their immediate anxieties and enable them to return to work. (Smith 1971, p.1)

Similarly, other patients directly counterpoised the personal challenge and therapeutic opportunities available at the day hospital with the passivity which they felt was induced by medical psychiatric treatment:

> Psychotherapy is painful. You have to face a lot of unpleasant things about yourself. In hospital you can remain completely docile. You're drugged and you sleep and you try not to think about anything. You're relegated to the role of a dependant child. (Paddington patient quoted in Benn 1972, p.40)

Patients appeared on TV and radio and were able to play a crucial role in the protest particularly as they were often able to carry out actions that would have been impossible for staff. For example, in February 1972 they took direct action and gatecrashed a meeting of the Regional Hospital Board to discuss the closure of the unit (Durkin 1972a, b). This freedom to take action was also possible for students who were on placement at Paddington. The social work student who was the campaign co-ordinator recalled:

> I was ideally placed to get the protest organised and everything, and to perhaps protect the staff from some of the flak from that, because as a student coming in I could really do that. (Davies 2000)

A demonstration and a parliamentary delegation and deputation to the Secretary of State, Keith Joseph, was planned. The action group made up a spurious date on which the decision on the transfer would be made. They circulated this date and informed journalists to try to pre-empt a decision in their favour and keep the momentum of the protest going. This strategy appeared to succeed. The decision about the transfer date was set for 11 April 1972, and the effectiveness of the campaign seemed to be such that the media and even the Board of Governors of St Mary's itself responded by this date. When the date arrived, the campaign co-ordinator called the Ministry to receive the decision about the day hospital and was informed that they would not be receiving any more deputations as the transfer proposal had been abandoned. On the same day, the Board of Governors of St Mary's informed the Department of Health and Social Security (DHSS) that they would not proceed with the transfer. They argued that in their view, the particular type of treatment given at the day hospital could not satisfactorily be assimilated into the psychiatric department at St Mary's. The DHSS subsequently withdrew their proposal and even agreed to some limited increases in staffing levels at the day hospital. It did seem that the protest had been victoriously successful and had saved the day hospital from incorporation and possible annihilation:

> The unit would have been quietly run down if there had not been an effective protest movement. To withdraw the proposals was the only way to prevent further publicity, especially that which would undoubtedly have followed the MPs delegation and the demonstration. (Ward 1972, p.18)

In these situations it is often unclear whether it was the protests themselves which stopped the transfer plans or other intervening factors. However, in many ways what was more important was that mounting the campaign became a highly empowering and validating experience for both patients and workers. For example, because the transfer proposal was withdrawn, the Secretary of State refused to meet the deputation that patients and staff had planned. This angered the campaigners who decided to go ahead with the deputation and demonstration anyway. The demonstration, which according to the local paper attracted about a hundred people, turned into a celebration with street play and folk singing. A song had even been written and this 'Paddington Protest' song was performed at the demonstration. The positive elements of the protests were due to the sense of strength and togetherness that it created and also resulted from the various debates and discussions that were held about how to develop the campaign.

## Protest debates

A strong sense of solidarity and shared purpose are essential elements to any campaign that hopes to win. From the outside campaigns appear solidly cohesive, yet if they have any hope of succeeding groups have to negotiate both the differences of their members, and the pressures of outside forces.

This process is not linear but is produced by the outcome of interaction, nego-tiation and oppositions between different orientations (Melucci 1995). Pad-dington was no different; the protest was successful but the process of cam-paigning was one of internal negotiation and debate. Here I want to highlight some of the debates that occurred during the campaign, and how different positions were occupied, negotiated and contested.

The struggle for the survival of Paddington became a battleground in which numerous interests and concerns were articulated (Kavalier 1972). In reading the various accounts of the protests it is hard to identify any single, clear and shared purpose or demand. While all participants agreed that the day hospital should not to be transferred and/or closed, the finer details and wider political aspirations differed significantly.

Concrete proposals from the campaign tended to focus on the need for resources for the day hospital. For example, Goodburn argued that any other provision should be in addition to, not instead of, the day hospital (1972). Over the previous five years it was felt that the Regional Hospital Board had run down the day hospital by leaving staff positions unfilled. Due to this, and the fact that Goodburn's position as a locum consultant was still temporary, one demand was for permanent staff. In this sense the focus was a much more straightforward one of defending public services rather than any more radical call for alternative principles and understandings of mental illness and psychi-atry.

However, the protests were more than this. Baron (1984a, b) argued that the protests were about preserving the day hospital as a therapeutic community. Certainly one of the invited speakers, Malcolm Pines, was invited specifically to comment on the importance of the group-based therapeutic community approach. At some points during the campaign, Paddington's identity as a therapeutic community was drawn upon to emphasise its radical and democratising potential. For example, one commentator asked: 'Are Ther-apeutic Communities like Paddington Day Hospital a possible threat to the hierarchy of the National Health Service?' (Ward 1972, p.18).

Indeed, shared decision-making was very much a part of the therapeutic community approach at the day hospital and did become one of the focal points for defence in the campaign. Staff and patients had some sense of control over the hospital and were used to taking part in decision-making. The lack of any meaningful consultation about the proposed transfer with staff or patients was acutely felt and became an important factor generating a sense of collective grievance. Thus another observer noted that 'Dr Goodburn and the nurses, other staff and patients felt that they had an interest, indeed a right, to have a say in what was going on with *their* hospital (Kavalier 1972, p.491).

However, the broader focus of the protest was eagerly contested, especially regarding how 'political' the campaign should be. Debates ensued about whether it should confine itself to the day hospital or focus on wider issues such as criticising psychiatry and its relationship to society. Many patients and other activists involved in the campaign favoured a more radical approach and generated the idea of calling the public meeting 'The Mad Society'.

Other campaigners wanted to appeal for wider support from other professionals, and did not want to alienate potential allies and supporters. Many of the more established politicians and reformers argued against what they saw as its 'politicisation' (Durkin 1972a, p.14). For example, the local MP Arthur Latham argued that it was not a 'political issue' but about whether the hospital was worth keeping open (Paddington Mercury 1972). This approach reflected a wider and less militant plea for social reform that was also taking place at the time. For example, the National Mind Campaign was launched in 1971 by the National Association for Mental Health (MIND). This campaign highlighted the lack of psychotherapy available within the NHS and supported a wide range of treatments, including ECT (Ennals 1973, p.7). David Ennals, MIND's first campaigns director was one of the more 'moderate' voices of the campaign. (Interestingly, by the time of the Paddington Inquiry in 1976, Ennals was the Secretary of State for Health and Social Services and therefore effectively presided over the closure of Paddington and the sacking of Goodburn.)

Eventually the title for the public meeting was agreed as 'Madness – a choice of treatment' emphasising the notion of 'choice' and treatment options (Smith 1972). This helped to focus the campaign on the right to long-term community psychotherapy on the NHS, rather than more short-term medicalised treatment. Yet it was also explicitly argued that it was important not to 'polarise the issue between psychodynamic and organic psychiatry' because 'there is a great need for both treatments' (Benn 1972, p.40). Thus Malcolm Pines, one of the invited speakers, reportedly argued the case for both types of treatment – those based on drugs and ECT, and alternatives such as therapeutic communities.

Despite this compromise, the more radical elements within the campaign continued to be influential. The campaign action group issued a statement indicating their opposition to ECT and drugs (Durkin and Douieb 1975, p.14). This radical approach coincided with the anti-palliative stance to medication that was being developed at the day hospital.

During the campaign, Paddington's status as a radical alternative grew and this endeared it to those interested in anti-psychiatry and other radical initiatives and causes. While the 'official' slogan for the campaign became 'The Madness of closing Paddington Day Hospital: Save the Choice of Treatment', an alternative slogan was also developed alongside it. This slogan, 'Paddington Day keeps madness at bay', was also circulated and appeared on posters and stickers around west London. This was suggested by one of the patients at Paddington and taken up by some of the campaigners who viewed it as an ironic commentary on the division between the 'mad' and the 'sane' and the idea that madness could be (or should be) contained within institutions. As one of the activists recalled:

> Every one of those people labelled a 'patient'...ended up in that role to keep other people's systems in place...and so once they were accepted in their own right, then all the implications for those other systems was very serious...that's where the phrase 'Paddington Day keeps madness at bay' is all about...I mean it's because of the way society needs these people to be at the hospitals here. (Davies 2000)

A similar idea and critique was also used in the Italian democratic psychiatry movement. Here the institution was seen as symbolic of the dynamic of exclusion and destroying the institution would force society to confront its exclusionary practices and confront its own contradictions by facing the so-called 'mad'. Working in the context of the Trieste initiative, Franco Basaglia had argued that the practice of therapeutic communities could be part of an increased understanding of how mental patients are scapegoats for a society riddled with internal contradictions (1987). The aim of the movement was to deprive society of the place that was created to internalise its contradictions, while at the same time finding new ways for the mad to be in society. The task of psychiatry would then become a politicised one in relation to society's relationship with madness.

Some of the more radical activists at Paddington reflected on how the wider authorities' decision to reverse the proposed transfer of the day hospital may actually have been taken to maintain this division. In other words, keeping the day hospital open was a way of containing the dissent, disquiet and anger that the patients were developing, which was partly unleashed by the threat of closure and protests. Ironically, in this scenario the protests were used by the authorities to secure what the more cautious campaigners wanted, an alternative to treating the madness of individuals, rather than a critique of prevailing social conditions. While the slogan 'Paddington Day keeps madness at bay' could have resulted in an idealisation of the day hospital itself, its intention was actually a wider critique of society and its need for such institutions in the first place. However, such commentary got lost and marginalised in the bid to save Paddington from closure. Meanwhile, the focus on Paddington as a pioneering individual institution placed a heavy burden of responsibility on the service and raised expectations that ultimately it was unable to fulfil.

Despite this, the resonance of the protests contributed to developments in consciousness and awareness both within and beyond the confines of the day hospital itself. The campaign sent out a powerful message regarding the strength of feeling around Paddington. The show of strength and solidarity around the campaign, and especially patients' involvement in it, was unprecedented and contributed to a wave of patients' unrest and dissatisfaction, both locally and nationally. Any successful campaign sends out a message of hope, inspiring confidence and feeding into other emerging campaigns and critiques. As one activist recalled:

> The key thing – when you think that – I mean the mental patients holding a meeting in the House of Commons… Has it ever happened since? I don't know, but it was absolutely unique then… It was absolutely unprecedented. And to be there, and to be heard, and to hold a very substantial meeting! The day they invaded the Regional Hospital Board, that was absolutely unprecedented as well. To go into a very high level meeting, to get into the premises, to go and sit down and refuse to move until they'd come and spoken to the people that it was all about… People respected that, the world was watching. (Davies 2000)

The importance, and indeed 'health', of evoking the 'lost potential for action' (Lomas 1987, p.118) has been highlighted by many theorists (see Cooper 1980; Coppock and Hopton 2000; Ernst and Goodison 1981; Estroff 1981; Fanon 1967, 1986; Holland 1992; Lomas 1987; Newman 1991; Podvoll 1991; Samuels 1993). For example, Estroff described the importance of patients taking political action in an American mental health centre:

> The exhilaration of hearing those individuals' demand services and attention and politicise rather than pathologise their needs… after that ritual of legitimisation…that experience confirmed for me that socio-political action is as necessary to progress for these people as caring, understanding, and innovative treatment programmes. (1981, p.272)

## Protest and the therapeutic community

The particular strength and effectiveness of the campaign also arose from the specific practices that were being developed at Paddington. Durkin argued that patients' participation in the protests specifically 'evolved from the ideology and functioning of the day hospital' (Durkin 1972a, p.13). We will therefore now take a look at how developing practices at the day hospital itself provided the impetus for the protests.

Rather than assuming that psychiatric patients' resistance was somehow waiting pre-formed, ready to be expressed, it may be that the development of collective working at the day hospital actually contributed to the creation of the conditions for greater solidarity and action. In a different context, Fantasia described how the internal dynamics of 'wild cat' industrial strikes created 'cultures of solidarity' during the negotiation of collective action (Fantasia 1988). He argued that these developed in the context of pre-existing patterns of active workgroup social relationships on the shop floor.

We could draw a parallel between this and the therapeutic community-based practices at Paddington, which helped to create the social basis of trust and mutuality on which group solidarity was dependent. Just as mutual co-operation is necessary to meet the demands of production in the labour process, so it is equally necessary for 'therapeutic work' in a therapeutic community. Such co-operation also provides a foundation for expressions of 'co-operative activity which may go beyond, and become independent of, the institutional boundaries which constrain them' (Fantasia 1988, p.108). This process was exemplified at Paddington in the formation of the Mental Patients Union, where patients developed more independent activity and self-organisation.

There were also other more specific aspects of the day hospital that con-tributed to the development of such a vigorous campaign. It was common practice at the hospital to examine patients' difficulties in relation to ongoing social situations, and their ability to challenge these situations was part of this examination (Durkin 1972a). This was part of the challenge to patients' passivity and patient status and was powerfully enacted through the protest. Thus it became part of 'therapy' to examine patients' own power in relation to the new external situation that threatened the existence of the day hospital (Durkin 1972a). It became apparent that the authorities were relying on this perceived passivity of patients to ensure an acceptance of the decision but the action group 'decided not to collude with such an expectation' (Durkin 1972a, p.14). We have already seen how the shared decision-making processes at the day hospital helped to ensure greater involvement in the campaign. Moreover, the campaign also drew upon the growing desire of staff and patients to expand their awareness of wider decision-making processes in society. As Goodburn argued:

> All concerned in the campaign have become increasingly aware of the lack of consultation that exists with the NHS, so that decisions tend to be taken by those in authority without sufficient consultation with those actually using the service, be they patients, referring agencies, or in this case, the staff of the unit. (1972, p.459)

At that time, this emphasis on challenging external structures of power converged with, and was justified through, a psychoanalytically influenced practice that viewed the understanding of 'here and now' individual and social relations as being crucial to transformation. Thus, rather than being seen as outside the remit of psychotherapy in the day hospital, the threat to its existence was seen as shared knowledge within the community as it was directly impacting upon social relations in the community. While this version of the importance of here and now interpersonal relations is not confined to psychoanalytic thinking, in this context it was possible to relate the emerging situation to psychoanalytic notions of transference relationships in the day hospital. This thinking helped justify a collective response to this new situation as part of the therapeutic process. As Goodburn (2000) recalled:

> Really all we have in common is the evidence we have before us now. Which is a very good, you know, justification for sticking to here and now transference, which I fail to do on many occasions I'm sure. But I mean that really is the discipline... It isn't the only evidence you've got, but it's the only evidence you've got in common... They were working collectively... So that any evidence which was accruing during the process of the protest was to be fed back into the common situation.

While this kind of thinking is not necessarily unusual in therapeutic community practices, what was most striking was the way that therapy was seen as being bound up with the material circumstances in which patients and staff found themselves. This politicised the whole therapeutic process as the protest campaign was viewed as therapy itself (Goodburn 1972). Goodburn argued that practices that ignored the realities of government organisations and administrative and wider power structures resulted in an incomplete therapeutic process (Haddon 1973). In the particular social milieu created at Paddington, for a short time, psychoanalytic thinking provided a helpful framework for understanding the connections between the individual, 'madness' and the wider society. This became possible through wider conditions of political possibility as patients and staff consciously made connections with a wider network of people who were also gaining politicised awareness and developing social action. However, when the protests and action died down, there was no longer a wider context through which to support such understandings and because psychoanalysis increasingly became the dominant framework, the day hospital was faced more directly with conflicts emerging out of this approach itself – as will be discussed later in this book.

## The protest and the wider context

> Five years earlier or later, the Save the Day Hospital Campaign would probably not have received the enthusiastic support it received in 1971. (Hall 1979, p.5)

While the success of the protest was partly inspired by the particular approach being developed at Paddington it can also be attributed to the wider climate of protest and the emergence of other social movements and organisations at that time. The threat of closure served to crystallise more general discontent. The 'New Left' and the women's movement were also becoming increasingly concerned about issues of identity, subjectivity, freedom and oppression. The politicisation of personal issues, symbolised by the slogan the 'personal is political', ensured the politicisation of the mental health field too.

The protests happened at just the time that an international patients' movement was beginning to emerge and at the peak of the popularity of anti-psychiatry. The initiation of radical organisations and initiatives in psychology, social work and psychiatry helped mobilisation and increased networks of activists. For example, the Politics of Psychology conference held at the London School of Economics in 1971 launched a number of radical psychology initiatives and alternative psychiatry groups such as People Not Psychiatry were set up (Barnett 1973). Also Case Con, a radical social work organisation, which played on the idea that social work 'case work' was a con trick, started in 1970. Many students inspired by the events of 1968 went into professions like social work wanting to act on some of the lessons learned through this period of heightened activism (Brown and Hanvey 1987). This, and the continuing wider politicised climate, ensured that health and welfare were to become politically contested arenas. Psychiatry, in particular, was a field that was ripe for a moment when a public manifestation of the conflicts between psychiatry and society could highlight some of the ongoing concerns expressed by patients, anti-psychiatry and radicalised workers. Melucci (1989) has described how periods of latent activism become visible when a field of public conflict arises.

The film *Family Life* went on release just at this time and it helped to provide fertile ground from which the campaign could grow by raising awareness and gaining outside support. *Family Life* told the story of Sue, a young woman scapegoated and psychiatrised by overbearing and confusing family circumstances. Sue was beginning to make progress in terms of her increasing awareness and steps towards independence at an alternative Laingian in-patient therapeutic community with a young progressive libertarian psychiatrist. However, following a meeting regarding the psychiatrist's future, the hospital board decided not to renew his contract and the radical community 'experiment' closed. This decision effectively condemned Sue to receiving harsh and punitive psychiatric treatment. After being silenced with a series of ECT treatments, she is paraded in front of a group a medical students as a 'typical example of a schizophrenic'. Leaflets were given out at screenings of *Family Life* and even the film-makers, Ken Loach and Tony Garnett, got involved in the Paddington campaign. Goodburn knew Loach previously, as they had attended the same school together in Birmingham, and he made contact with Loach as the campaign began to take off.

The parallel seemed obvious. So much so that although the film had been heavily influenced by David Cooper's therapeutic community, Villa 21 at Shenley Hospital (Cooper 1967), some thought at the time that the film was actually based on Paddington. The film seemed to mirror the situation at the day hospital and drove home the possible outcome for young women like Sue if the campaign failed and the day hospital closed. Just as Loach's film *Cathy Come Home* helped fuel public interest, discontent and outrage about homelessness culminating in the development of the charity Shelter in 1966, *Family Life* provided an important reference point and aid to public consciousness and awareness about the developing politicisation of mental health.

Further evidence of this wave of social change is apparent from other protests in psychiatry across Europe and the US. For example, a series of progressive and politicised group work sessions with psychiatric patients had begun with the help of Wolfgang Huber at the Heidelberg Day Hospital during the late 1960s. When Huber was sacked, patients held a 'general assembly' opposing his dismissal, which was later claimed to be the first genuine patients' assembly in the history of psychiatry (Spandler 1992). Out of these protests the Socialist Patient Collective (SPK) was formed in 1970–1971 (Kotowicz 1997; Spandler 1992; SPK 1972, 1993). While it is unclear how much the SPK explicitly utilised therapeutic community ideas, its development was kick-started through a protest to save Huber and the radical elements of the day hospital.

Cross-fertilisation between Paddington and other developing networks helped to develop this potential for mental health activism beyond the Paddington protests, inspiring other initiatives and organisations. The radical anti-psychiatry group COPE (the Campaign for the Organisation of Psychiatric Emergencies) like the MPU, was formed in 1973. COPE was particularly strong in West London and took some of its inspiration from the Paddington protests. In June 1973 a group calling itself the 'Campaign for Psychotherapy Survival' was set up to oppose the closure of an in-patient psychotherapy group at Hill End Hospital, St Albans. This group also drew inspiration from the Paddington Campaign (Copeman 1973).

The protests brought together previously disparate strands of anti-psychiatry alongside other emerging challenges and growing political awareness and action that was developing at the time both within and beyond psychiatry. The most significant organisation to emerge from the events at Paddington was the Mental Patients Union and these events helped to kick-start a national patient's movement. It is this that we go on to consider in Chapter 4.

# CHAPTER FOUR

# The Mental Patients Union

The most important outcome of the ambitions ignited during the Paddington protests was the development of a national network known as the Mental Patients Union (MPU). The MPU was an organisation of mental patients and their allies who campaigned and organised against psychiatric treatment and incarceration. Although there has been resistance to psychiatry ever since its inception, such resistance has rarely been documented (Campbell 1996; Crossley 1999a). However, we do know that back in 1620 the inmates of Bedlam petitioned Parliament about their treatment (Seeger 1996) and in 1846 the Alleged Lunatics Friends Society (ALFS) was formed to highlight the legal rights of detained patients (Hervey 1986; Perceval 1961). However, the formation of a social movement is usually located at the point at which a large, collective, political movement of some force emerges, broadening its aim from a focus on parliamentary reform to a wider challenge to prevailing social and cultural perceptions about the issue in question. For example, the AFLS focused on a legal struggle for certain individuals not to be labelled insane and campaigned against their incarceration. Groups like the MPU moved towards a broader focus which challenged the very existence of madness itself and the ways in which particular groups of people were pathologised in the psychiatric system. Following on from this, newer organisations such as Mad Pride have sought to celebrate the very existence of 'madness' and their subjugated identity and culture.

Many commentators locate the MPU as a pivotal organisation that marked the beginning of the organised survivor movement in Britain because it paved the way for subsequent survivor or user groups and other organisations to emerge (Curtis *et al.* 2000). The MPU has also been characterised as one of the first organisations in the UK to explicitly politicise mental health (Crossley 1999a; Curtis *et al.* 2000). This chapter outlines the development of the MPU specifically *à propos* its relationship with, and divergence from, its initial roots at Paddington.

# The formation of the Mental Patients Union

There are a number of interrelated ways in which Paddington helped to fuel the development of the MPU and we need to examine these connections. First, the confidence and organisational skills that participants developed during the protests provided much of the inspiration for the MPU. Second, other emerging radical ideas and organisations fuelled its inception. Finally, it became more possible to organise through the collectivised and libertarian environment of the day hospital. Early activists in the MPU clearly linked the formation of the MPU to their experiences at Paddington:

> Paddington Day Hospital made the Mental Patients Union possible, abso-lutely, there's no doubt about that. Without Paddington there would have been no MPU, there's no doubt about that. I mean, well, there might have been something else, but there wouldn't have been MPU. (Douieb 2000)

Mike Lawson was a Paddington patient who became an active member in the MPU, a path that led him to become the Vice-chair of national MIND in the 1980s. He reflected on how 'the seeds of the MPU were planted at Padding-ton Day Hospital because it was carried through from a caucus which was formed at the Paddington' (Lawson 1999). This caucus began with a small group of staff and patients at Paddington who were inspired by the successful campaign and continued to meet at the day hospital to discuss ideas and formulate future plans. One concrete outcome of these discussions was a document called *The Need for a Mental Patients Union* and this was circulated in December 1972 as a pamphlet (Durkin 1973; Durkin and Douieb 1975).

The pamphlet specifically developed many of the ideas that had formed during the campaign and described the Paddington protest as the first and only example of realised patient power in this country (MPU 1972). The doc-ument was written by four individuals who were involved in the Paddington campaign. Although they described themselves as an ad hoc pilot committee of mental patients and ex-patients, Eric Irwin was the only current Paddington patient in the original committee who was actually named on the original pamphlet. Lesley Mitchell was a junior Occupational Therapist at Padding-ton, Liz Durkin was a social work student at Paddington and Brian Douieb was a local activist who became involved through the campaign.

Despite Irwin's long-time institutionalisation within conventional psy-chiatric institutions (he was known to suffer from Tardive Dyskinesia, a long-term side-effect of neuroleptic anti-psychotic medication), he was described as an articulate, deep-thinking Marxist and was viewed by the others as the biggest inspiration for the development of the MPU. Irwin was to become a tireless campaigner and anti-psychiatry activist, later being referred to as an 'elder statesmen of patients' rights' (Bangay 1988). During an interview in *Asylum* magazine a year before he died, Irwin recalled:

> I got involved in the movement with the aim of keeping open a day hospital which was threatened with closure way back in 1972. The campaign by the staff and patients was successful. It was after that they decided something more radical ought to be done. (Quoted in Van de Graaf 1989a, p.5)

The network of activists created in the campaign provided important informal leadership in the early days of the MPU. The following lengthy account illustrates how the protests helped tap into the growing awareness and imagination of patients and other activists galvanised by other radical ideas of the time, and how this resulted in the realisation of a patients union:

> I mean what happened was, as I remember it...there were early discussions with people [patients] like Eric and Michael about the issues that arose from the protest...and general political discussions about things. And we were getting information from other mental patients in the country... I think it was the realisation that, well, not exactly Paddington, but why can't we have an organisation...that consolidates that power... One of the things we wanted to challenge was the Mental Health Act 1959. It was a horrendous piece of legislation, which gave patients no rights whatsoever. Plus there was the whole process of labelling, and people's own low opinion of themselves... And, of course, there were lots of other things that were going on. There was awareness from the womens' movement; there was awareness from the black movement. People saying, 'Look, here I am, I'm black, I'm a woman, you know, I'm proud to be who I am.' And then you got people [at Paddington] saying, 'We're mental patients, we're proud to be who we are... We have a role in relation to the means of production and social class and all the rest of it'... I think actually it was Eric that said, 'Well, you know, let's consolidate it and have some sort of organisation which pronounces that pride...that there is a way forward' and out of that came the Mental Patients Union. (Douieb 2000)

The previous chapter described how, in the face of threats to the day hospital, the traditional passive patient role was questioned. This seemed to exemplify the Paddington practice of refusing to collude with dominant expectations and labelling of psychiatric patients. The MPU developed these ideas further by trying to examine the social, economic and political function of the role of the 'mental patient':

The whole idea of MPU was for people to challenge that really, or to look at very closely at what and who they were and what they were doing within society... The MPU was able to say 'Well, you know, let's look at this labelling process, let's look at your role within society. What role do you play?' And you actually play a very useful role for society, you know because society needs deviants, and mental patients are brilliant deviants. (Douieb 2000)

The group drew attention to the way in which an individual's valid attempts to deal with the distress or disturbance caused by particular social circumstances can be misunderstood as illness and psychiatrised. Developing this idea they put the following (adapted) quote from the US psychiatrist and psychoanalyst Karl Menninger on the cover of the MPU pamphlet, alongside a picture of a fish caught on a hook:

An individual having unusual difficulties in coping with his environment struggles and kicks up the dust, as it were. I have used the figure of a fish caught on a hook: his gyrations must look peculiar to other fish that don't understand the circumstances; but his splashes are not his affliction, they are his effort to get rid of his affliction and as every fisherman knows these efforts may succeed. (Menninger, quoted in MPU 1972, p.1)

The symbolism resulted in the document being popularly known in the movement as the 'fish pamphlet'. A similar theme of an individual being caught or trapped was articulated in other arenas and culminated in the MPU adopting as their logo a symbol of a human head caught in a spider's web (Crossley 1999a). This clearly marked and named the oppression that accompanied much psychiatric intervention. More than this, the group argued that through recognising common experiences of this oppression it created interpersonal connections and a solidarity that could forge a willingness to actively challenge that oppression:

The Mental Patients Union was about self-empowering but it was also about self-supporting. And of course there is that line from [Leonard] Cohen... 'I've been where you're hanging and I think I can see how you're pinned' ...I mean that encapsulates exactly really what the MPU was about, and in fact all self-help groups really from that time onwards really used that ethos. (Douieb 2000)

The 'fish pamphlet' set out the case for the MPU and the group grew in strength, with the addition of other patients, ex-patients and activists from Paddington and beyond. They decided to distribute posters to mental hospitals, day centres and hostels advertising a first public meeting called 'Is psychiatry social repression?: The case for a Mental Patients Union'. This meeting, in March 1973, was held at Paddington Day Hospital and effectively launched the MPU as a national organisation. To the surprise of the organisers, it became an unprecedented event with over 150 people attending, more than 100 of whom were reportedly patients or ex-patients (Durkin and Douieb 1975). People who attended came from all over the country, including Leeds, Birmingham and Southampton. Two activists recalled how people had even managed to escape from hospital to attend. Patients were recorded as coming from special hospitals such as Broadmoor and Rampton, as well as other therapeutic communities such as Shenley and Malborough Day (Durkin 1972b). Participants had heard about the meeting through political networks that were tapped into and developed through the protests.

The rapid development of the MPU was informed by some of the lessons learnt at Paddington during the protests, for example, the use of publicity, the media, and other contacts and networks. Furthermore, attendance was boosted by a BBC Radio Four programme, which had interviewed activists the night before (Crossley 1999a).

> That network, you know, all the card index boxes full of press contacts and people all over the country that supported it…that was all in place for MPU. It had it ready-made…that there were so many people who knew each other and had already developed relationships with each other. So…there was a group of people already made. (Davies 2000)

The MPU can be seen as a consolidation of the spirit and success engendered during the protest. The high-profile political campaign at Paddington brought discussion of psychiatric issues into a wider public arena, which opened up the possibilities for transposing radical politics on to the mental health field. Activities at Paddington tapped into a wider mood of dissatisfaction and critique within psychiatry and a more generalised culture of resistance outside psychiatry. Not only was there an emerging audience for protest in mental health, but change seemed possible. The protests have been described as a 'key trigger event' or 'spark' that ignited the movement and was clearly an inspiration for the MPU (Crossley 1999a). The process of organising the campaign extended the consciousness of the participants and opened up a space in which the MPU could exist, when 'reaction gave way to pro-action and the idea of a permanent "union" for "mental patients" emerged' (Crossley 1999a, p.653).

In addition, it has been argued that a pre-existing communicational network or infrastructure is the primary prerequisite for seemingly 'spontaneous' social action (Freeman 1999). These, often informal, networks need to be 'co-optable' into the new ideas of an emerging movement. Such networks can be galvanised into a new movement by a specific strain or crisis when they are effectively mobilised by organisers seeking to create new movements (Freeman 1999). Incipient new movements need to interpret common experiences and perceptions that are formed through radical communities, in ways that point out channels for social action (Freeman 1999). This happened through the Paddington protests and then through a concrete demand for a patients' union.

In reflecting on the successful protest at Paddington, Crossley suggested that encouraging service users to form a union could be viewed as a radicalisation of the standard organisational and pedagogic role of the social worker (Crossley 1999a). Similarly, the organisation of independent patient activity, critique and social action might be viewed as a logical extension or radicalisation of the standard collectivised therapeutic role of the therapeutic community. For example, one article explicitly linked 'patient power', not with the TC approach *per se*, which can be 'as authoritarian as organic methods' (Durkin 1972a, p.13), but with the particular radicalised version of a TC developed at Paddington.

Yet during this period the therapeutic community movement was an important part of a wider communicational network of ideas and practices of resistance and alternatives to psychiatry. This could be referred to as a 'radical community' where like-minded progressive ideas and people circulate and interact (Freeman 1999, p.18). Therapeutic communities played an important role in the vision of an alternative future, both inside and outside psychiatry, following the culture of resistance post-May 1968. They were influenced by the progressive ideas of the time and were often seen as one of the few genuine alternatives to hospital-based, biomedical psychiatry. Moreover, therapeutic communities were about questioning, confrontation and change, evoking notions of freedom and liberation. These qualities are precisely those deemed necessary for a 'radical community' (Freeman 1999). The following description of the communicational origins of social movements highlights a potential parallel with therapeutic community practices:

> From their own experiences, directly and concretely, people feel the need for change in a situation that allows for an exchange of feelings with others, mutual validation, and a subsequent reinforcement of innovative interpretation. (p.22)

For these reasons, it is perhaps not that surprising that a therapeutic community was the most likely setting in which the MPU could have developed. It is unclear how much the protests themselves, rather than Paddington as a therapeutic community, inspired the development of the MPU. However, what seemed to be important was the libertarian structure of Paddington, which was open to radical alternative ideas and allowed for such developments to take place. Facilitating the convening of meetings, some of which led to the formation of the MPU, was part of the approach fostered in the day hospital. Patients (and staff) were able to use the facilities of the day hospital to develop new initiatives over and above the roles and involvement usually expected of each party. This included fostering links with other progressive organisations outside the day hospital.

One activist reflected that without the consultant Goodburn actually 'opening the doors we would never actually have met' (Douieb 2000). Although Goodburn went to the first MPU meeting and recalled having 'some sympathy' with the MPU patients, he knew little of subsequent developments and very clearly took a back seat in the MPU. However, while he was never actively involved in the MPU, he would regularly put patients in contact with them.

> He certainly was very supportive of it, and I remember he put all sorts of people our way that came to him, and he would say, 'No, go and talk to MPU about it'... He would say to me 'you can organise this meeting, you can do this union' and then that left him to be doing all the action at his level, with all his meetings, and all the politics that went on at his level, so I wouldn't have expected him to be that involved. (Davies 2000)

An examination of the relevance of Paddington to the development of the MPU helps to identify the elements within a therapeutic community that may help or hinder the development of progressive initiatives. However, at the same time it is important to acknowledge that both Paddington and the MPU were part of a much broader social impetus for change within psychiatry and therapeutic practice. While activists were developing the MPU at Paddington, other similar groups were forming around the country and elsewhere.

As we have already noted, the Socialist Patients Collective in Heidelberg, Germany, developed in 1971, and a number of radical patients' organisations were developing in Canada and the USA (such as the Mental Patients Association in Vancouver, the Mental Patients Political Action Committee in New York and the Mental Patients Liberation Project in Denver). In addition the Scottish Union of Mental Patients (SUMP) was actually set up in 1971. SUMP was quite a small, relatively short-lived organisation set up by a number of patients in Hartwood Hospital (MPU 1974). Key members of SUMP, such as Tom Ritchie and Robin Farquason, went on to help develop the MPU in London. In fact, what was remarkable was how different patient unions were developing around the country, often seemingly unbeknownst to each other.

More fundamentally, the emerging patients' movement was given impetus by other political challenges to prevailing social structures and institutions and the wider counter-cultural climate. Thus, some of the leading members of the MPU had been activists in other organisations such as the Claimants Union, PROP (Protection of the Rights of Prisoners), the Fabian Society and the International Socialists. A new generation of patients and workers were influenced by these other struggles and were given the opportunity of bringing these challenges into the mental health field via events such as the threat to Paddington.

## Surfing the wave: the MPU after Paddington

> Paddington was the beginning, it was the tidal wave, if you like, and MPU was able to ride that wave, to surf that wave, getting bigger as it went along. (Douieb 2000)

The MPU suffered a number of setbacks in its early development, for example the death of one key early MPU member Robin Farquarson, who died in a fire shortly after the first MPU meeting. Despite this, the MPU demonstrated that it was not dependent on just a few members as has been suggested elsewhere (Rogers and Pilgrim 1991). It continued and grew at an impressive rate developing numerous branches all over the country, in many cases led by patients and ex-patients themselves.

The MPU soon developed an autonomous life of is own. While in the early days of the MPU, Paddington played an important part in terms of its membership and meetings, by the mid-1970s this was no longer the case. MPU membership increased rapidly and the organisation quickly became a national network establishing numerous local offshoots. Many major cities had the benefit of an active MPU. The second AGM was held in Manchester in March 1974, where a decision was taken to form a loose federation. Local groups worked autonomously, developing in accordance with local needs, issues and personalities.

Following its inception, the MPU developed a wide range of activities. These included setting up its own headquarters and developing 'crash houses' for people to stay when in crisis to avoid hospitalisation and psychiatric intervention. In addition, the MPU provided an advice and information service; advocated on behalf of patients in hospital; provided advice and representation at Mental Health Tribunals; and held MPU meetings on psychiatric wards. They also produced regular newsletters and information regarding patients' legal rights and the side-effects of psychiatric drugs and produced a comprehensive 'Declaration of Intent' and 'Drugs Charter' (e.g. Hill, Martin and Roberts 1975). The MPU made links with other socio-political issues of the time such as inadequate housing, women's oppression and psychiatry's complicity in the exploitation of the working class by ensuring people's compliance with damaging working conditions. In addition, just at the time when the British media and Western psychiatry were being alerted to Russia's use of psychiatric treatment as political repression, the MPU also highlighted some of the similarities between Western and Soviet psychiatry.

Furthermore, the MPU developed links with other national and international patients' groups that were developing in the USA and Europe. Activists from the MPU attended European conferences and had connections with patients' groups in France, Holland, Germany, Canada and the USA (Durkin and Douieb 1975). A group of activists from the UK brought a key document back from the German Socialist Patients' Collective in order to translate and circulate it (Spandler 1992; SPK 1972).

The first MPU document, the 'fish pamphlet', was heavily influenced by Marxist ideas and the MPU took class issues seriously. Indeed, the idea of a 'union' of mental patients clearly drew upon the idea of the collectivisation of workers in struggle, that patients were potentially part of a revolutionary working class, and highlighted the importance and possibilities of developing links with wider class forces:

> We looked at ourselves in relation to the social classes, and in relation to our role in society, and the relation to the means of production, so you get the concept of a union, you get the concept of us actually having union rights. We actually approached the TUC... [But] they weren't in the slightest bit interested! (Douieb 2000)

As the MPU grew, various positions on political and psychotherapeutic alternatives became keenly debated topics. The MPU was marked by a tension that mirrored a division in the broader 'anti-psychiatry' movement. This division was illustrated by the debate about whether to provide psychotherapy or a political critique of society and psychiatry. In a discussion of the US radical psychiatry movement, Castel et al. (1982) analysed the splits that developed between those continuing to use more 'radical' therapy in order to reform and humanise institutions, and those who wanted to move into a critique of the possibility of radical therapy itself. Tensions like these have plagued many radical social movements, not least the TC movement.

Crozier 1979; Ellison 1976; Goodburn 1986; Hinshelwood 1977; Millard 1985) and in the profession of group analysis (Ahlin 1981; Cooklin 1981; Kennard 1982; Kreeger 1981; Lemlij *et al.* 1982; Roberts 1982; Sandison 1982; Whiteley 1982, 1988). Accounts about the Paddington events were also written up in a number of unpublished papers (Crocket 1978; Goodburn 1977; Hall 1979; Lemlij *et al.* 1979) and the dispute gained local and national news coverage. Numerous debates developed after the demise of Paddington and these even included philosophical reflections regarding the nature of truth, the relationship between social and psychological ontology and epistemology (Millard 1985).

First, we need to know why Paddington developed in the way that it did. I aim to demonstrate that although this development may have contributed to its ultimate crisis and breakdown, there were some good reasons for the particular practice that was developed at Paddington, which have been lost in subsequent accounts. We will also see how staff responded to the challenges presented to them and the ideas and influences they drew upon to do so, specifically describing the influence of Henry Ezriel's psychoanalysis. Finally, we see how, despite good intentions, Paddington made insufficient attempts to understand how wider social determinants impacted on the community – factors that they were ill-equipped to deal with through relying on psychoanalysis alone.

## Emerging philosophy of practice at Paddington

During the period of protest Paddington was seen as an exciting and beneficial place by patients and workers. Referral rates were high, as was patient attendance at the various groups and meetings in the community. The tendency of numbers of referrals and attendees to rise during a public campaign has been documented elsewhere (Robinson 1994); however, as time elapsed, patients started to express their disillusionment through generally diminished attendance (Goodburn 1986). Events at Paddington after the protest both echoed changes that were occurring nationally and also expressed the patient and staff experience of political action and the difficulties of developing and sustaining a radical practice. In a national context, interest in TCs generally began to decline. In part this was because policies of 'community care', spurred on by critiques of traditional mental hospitals, fiscal constraints and the growing influence of the pharmaceutical industry, meant that acute psychiatry and short-stay, brief medicalised interventions became the norm. Low attendance and declining referrals to TCs reinforced a belief that they were under-used and therefore often recommended for closure (Hall 1979).

To deal with this tension, the MPU gradually disassociated itself from any association with any *specific* political or psychiatric 'alternative', in favour of concentrating on highlighting patients' rights such as resisting certain treatments and incarceration (Crossley 1999a). If we return to the parallel made in the previous chapter, between cultures of solidarity in industry and psychiatric institutions, this move was necessary. Social action can only embody transformative potential when it is able to achieve a degree of independence from the institutional structures that have been set up to contain it (Fantasia 1988).

> [The MPU] moved away very rapidly from Paddington, so that it wasn't associated with any kind of establishment psychiatry, radical or not, you know. It was very definitely a separate organisation. (Douieb 2000)

Although the right to have psychotherapy and the maintaining of Paddington as a TC were important demands in the Paddington campaign, the MPU went on to become critical of all therapeutic alternatives, including TCs (Durkin and Douieb 1975). It aimed to set up places of refuge 'without treatment, therapy or hierarchies' (Durkin and Douieb 1975, p.187). Psychotherapy was often viewed as brainwashing, individualistic and conformist (Durkin and Douieb 1975, p.189).

Although the MPU was formed through cultures of solidarity that developed in the organisation of the campaign to defend Paddington as a therapeutic community, it was further fuelled by of a growing sense of internal threats to democracy in Paddington and TCs generally. A critique of TCs was articulated even at the first national meeting of the MPU:

> In particular those in units with patients' committees believed themselves to have power already although they were challenged by other patients as to the real extent of their power, i.e. in seeing case-notes, when they could discharge themselves and other decisions in the unit. (Durkin and Douieb 1975, p.181)

Moreover, by distancing itself away from Paddington the MPU facilitated a questioning of therapeutic alternatives in general:

> Once away from it people began to talk more – maybe more critical of psychotherapy as a model, than had happened within Paddington itself...people had lots of their own stories to tell...about how they'd suffered from psychotherapy, as well as other treatments. (Davies 2000)

The psychotherapeutic practices developed at Paddington both facilitated the development of the MPU, and yet, as we shall see in the next chapter, diverged from the focus and demands of the MPU. The actual power that patients exercised at Paddington was questioned and viewed as only participation, falling short of patient control (Durkin and Douieb 1975). Thus the MPU developed to some extent in the context of, and in response to, the *limitations* of practices of 'radical therapy', particularly its utilisation of psychoanalysis:

> I suppose in a way you can think of it as an antithesis of psychotherapy, psychoanalysis I suppose, because that's all about going internally and MPU was all about going external...providing therapy for people by actually getting involved in social action. (Douieb 2000)

While the MPU became more antagonistic to, and distanced from, formal therapeutic alternatives, other 'anti-psychiatric' organisations were embracing various, usually 'humanistic', therapeutic strategies, such as co-counselling, encounter groups and Primal Scream (Hughes 1986). Although some of the key patients involved in radical initiatives came from a therapeutic community background, very few of those radical organisations advocated therapeutic community practices as a viable alternative. Although one organisation, COPE (the Campaign for the Organisation of Psychiatric Emergencies), which had also been inspired by the events at Paddington developed links with organisations such as the Philadelphia and the Arbours Associations. These organisations promote therapeutic communities influenced by radical psychiatrists such as Joseph Berke, Leon Redler and R.D. Laing as well as psychoanalysis (Claytor 1993). One key MPU activist commented that although the MPU crash houses had gained some insights from practices developed at Paddington, the approach could be better described as 'client-centred' and Rogerian – perhaps indicating how humanistic and person-centred approaches sit more comfortably with patient-led initiatives (Proctor 2002).

At the same time, the way that psychoanalytic thinking was used in the radicalised context of the day hospital did contribute to the development of particular group dynamics and new ways of thinking that, while far from creating the MPU, did help its initial development. Remember that the symbol of a 'fish on a hook', which was important in the formation of the MPU, was inspired by a quote from the psychoanalyst Karl Menninger. Indeed, Menninger's (and Laing's) ideas about the possibility of personal growth through psychosis also played a role in inspiring Soteria House (Mosher, Hendrix and Fort 2004). How far this inspiration was necessarily psychoanalytical in nature is unclear. However, the useful convergence of ideas in these examples might be due to the provocative nature of psychoanalytic discourse, which (particularly in the context of a TC) can develop group dynamics and understandings in unpredictable ways and, at least at Paddington, lead to social action.

# Thinking the impossible: the impact of the MPU

The MPU played a crucial part in spearheading a new social movement and this section reviews the impact of the MPU as a social movement organisation. Progressive social movements are vital sources of critique and innovation in modern societies (Crossley 1999a; Habermas 1987; Melucci 1996). They question social norms and values and challenge dominant power interests. In addition, social movements can transform individuals and social relationships. The MPU enabled the generation of new ideas, ideals, and ways of thinking and acting in relation to psychiatry. It articulated numerous discontents and mobilised large numbers of people who formed a new movement that expressed pride and dignity and enabled others to mobilise.

The MPU achieved one of the most important aims of a social movement: the extension of the realms of political possibility – or what has been called 'the art of creating the possible from the impossible' (Esteva 1999, p.174). An example of a situation that helped to create these conditions, alongside the energy and enthusiasm that was apparent in the early days of the MPU, is illustrated in the following account from a member of the MPU:

> What you remember is that it was just so open to people's ideas. And when you think…people have been labelled mentally ill… They had the most amazing ideas. Ideas no other people would even ever dared think. And yet everything was, 'OK, let's go with it, let's try it, let's do it.' You know, I mean like Pam with her flat, her squat, and [she said] 'this can be the office.' And we thought, 'Oh, what sort of place is this going to be? Will it be stable? And is it a good place to leave all our things?' And then we went there and it was just wonderful… She'd got this squat and – [it was] beautiful, she'd got everything out of skips, and she'd built things and made things, and everything was, you know, created by her…we just felt so comfortable in it. We had some of the early meetings there…and we wrote things there. (Davies 2000)

The MPU actively negotiated the creation of alternative meanings by explicitly challenging and deconstructing discourses and practices of psychiatry. Therefore the MPU achieved another important function of social movements, 'the elaboration in daily life of alternative meanings for individual and collective behaviour' (Melucci 1995, p.107). Although social-movement theory has theorised the growth and development of movements, it has rarely documented the frequently complex, yet crucial, experience of *becoming* radicalised. This process is frequently left implicit or assumed. Yet it is these, often hidden and overlooked, activities that help give rise to more visible and public action. Mike Lawson (1999) remembered the fear and excitement he associated with his growing politicisation during his time at Paddington and as a member of the MPU:

> Paddington Day Hospital was a great launch pad for me but was also terrifying because to become politicised is a terrifying thing...in the attempt to identify where one is within the power systems, the shock of even trying to find out is very dangerous, Pandora's box... It's catalysing the movement from victim to survivor and this is the most powerful jolt one ever really gets.

He vividly recalled an important turning point for him that occurred through a simple, but effective, piece of communication between himself and Eric Irwin:

> Through Eric I learned to question, first of all the diagnosis, and secondly my actual focus on life. It was through Eric and the Paddington Day Hospital experience, but through the recipients mainly, that I got politicised... All the raw material had accrued but I had no intellectual whereabouts... It was simply that Eric said 'what are you doing here?' and I said 'I'm a schizophrenic' and he said '*are you?*' That got me thinking the impossible... It seemed almost too cheeky to contemplate that in fact I, as an individual, am not ill, I'm actually being done over. Part of me had always felt this but to be able to assimilate what's going on and to actually give it some form in my way of perceiving things, seemed almost too good to be true... But the moment you get to that place you get other problems starting, which is how do you practicalise your newfound knowledge and this is the most difficult thing. If you've been constantly been kicked and you begin to realise that your situation is as someone who's been politically oppressed – to waken up to that blows your mind. (Lawson 1999)

It was such challenges to fundamentally held belief systems about mental illness and psychiatry that were encouraged in practices at Paddington, and then developed further in the MPU. Up until this time the dominant representation of most mental patients' accounts were focused around pleading the uniqueness of their individual situation as separate from that of other mental patients. Such accounts made a distinction between sanity and madness, and particular individuals pleaded their particular case for how they were not mad and thereby wrongly certified. The MPU helped to generate the notion of a common identity of oppression and also a sense of pride. It has been noted how psychiatric survivors' accounts have changed over the years from an individualised to a collectivised voice. Between the 1950s and the 1990s Crossley and Crossley (2001) show a distinct change in the way that patients voiced and portrayed their experiences. These changes were illustrated in the language used by patients which shifted from 'shame' to 'pride'; 'plea' to 'rights' and from 'I' to 'we'. They credit social movement organisations, and specifically the MPU, as having a significant impact on enabling these changes (Crossley and Crossley 2001).

Rather than relying on psychological notions of 'internal states' to describe this change, Crossley has called this the development of a radical 'habitus', a sociological term borrowed from Pierre Bourdieu (Crossley 1999a; Crossley and Crossley 2001). The process of political campaigning at Paddington challenged the self-awareness of mental patients and their role in society and 'shook up' the burgeoning radical habitus of participants. The actions of social movement organisations such as the MPU live on in the changes they bring about in both the skills and dispositions of activists (their habitus) and the social practices and fields they challenge (i.e. psychiatry):

> The activists today continue the traditions developed by the MPU, inheriting the habitus and field that the history of struggle has forged...the changed conditions and dispositions of action that their successors will inherit...lend continuity to life and to struggle, ensuring that history need never and can never start again. (Crossley 1999a, p.668)

This radical consciousness may, for periods of time, remain relatively dormant and un-exercised. However, it is 'always stored among people, and can, and will be, accessed later' (Burton 2000, p.23). It comprises a living tradition through the lived experience and embodied consciousness of activists and participants who 'pass on' their history, experiences and theory developed through social action. The existence and memory of the MPU has been carried on by a number of important activists who played an important role in transmitting a culture of resistance and keeping alive this radical tradition.

## The legacy of the MPU

Although the MPU folded by the late 1970s, there was a continuation of activists and networks which changed and metamorphosed into organisations that are still in existence today. There has been a small, but consistent, continuity of membership between the early 1970s and the mid-1980s when many argue that the user movement really established itself via the Nottingham Advocacy Group and Survivors Speak Out, which began in early 1986 (Campbell 1996, 1999; Rogers and Pilgrim 1991). In terms of membership, it is possible to draw a direct lineage from the MPU through to PROMPT (Protection of the Rights of Mental Patients in Treatment/

Therapy) to CAPO (Campaign against Psychiatric Oppression) to current groups like Survivors Speak Out, the Self Harm Network and the Hearing Voices Network.

The continuing importance of the MPU has been recognised in a number of ways. In a socio-historical analysis of post-war mental health movements, Crossley (1999a) places the importance of the MPU on a par with anti-psychiatry and MIND (the National Association for Mental Health). More specifically, CAPO (the Campaign against Psychiatric Oppression), which formed after the MPU had ceased, re-created large elements of the 'fish pamphlet' in its literature, and adopted the spider's web symbol. In addition, recent radical organisations loosely based around the notion of 'Mad Pride' specifically relate their historical and theoretical heritage back to the Mental Patients Union. The importance of this heritage was illustrated through the re-publication of the 'fish pamphlet' by Mad Pride, who argued that it is of great historical and political importance (Irwin et al. 2000). It was published as a timely reminder of the roots of the movement and helped set the context for a groundbreaking anthology of writings on mad culture and madness (Curtis et al. 2000).

The ongoing legacy of Paddington and the MPU can be also illustrated with reference to a recent short film narrated by Mike Lawson called 'fish on a hook' where some of the central ideas discussed here were re-articulated:

> It is rather like a fish wriggling on the end of a hook. So, initially one might think Mike's wriggling in this way and it makes no sense at all, he's doing a crazy dance. Until you see the hook in my gullet, and then its starts making sense. So I think a lot of us are wriggling and that's seen as a kind of illness. Without the vision of the hooks that we are bound by it seems that our behaviour is very crazy. But when seen in context it isn't. (Glynne 2003)

Organisations like Mad Pride are a re-emergence of more politicised elements of the psychiatric survivors' movement and reach back to ideas expressed more explicitly in the MPU, in terms of its Marxist influences, non-partisan political stance and its utilisation of direct action, notions of civil rights and 'pride'. Such organisations have criticised the incorporation and de-politicisation of what is now known as the 'service user movement' (Armes 2000). The more mainstream user movement has tended to eschew more oppositional and political stances in favour of more collaborative, entrist, reformist and consumerist strategies (Forbes and Sashidharan 1997; Thompson 1995).

In summary, rather than necessarily solving the ongoing tensions between a psychotherapeutic enquiry and political critique, there was a transitory synthesis during the Paddington protest and its immediate aftermath. By referring to this as a 'synthesis', I do not mean a collapsing of all conflicts and tensions, but rather that contradictions are played out in such a way that a new idea or understanding is forged that may transcend these oppositions in new and different ways. These forces brought to life new organisations and new understandings that have had enduring effects on the history and consciousness of radical mental health movements.

However, the synthesis that resulted from the struggle at Paddington was short-lived and not repeated. The protests not only helped provide the impetus for initiatives such as the MPU but also created a situation of enforced unity where differences became blurred and important conflicts and tensions were suppressed. In particular, Paddington increasingly resorted to psychoanalytically inspired means to challenge the identity of patients as passive recipients of services. In this context, it was perhaps ironic that patients themselves often resisted this practice by demanding certain rights and entitlements afforded to them as 'patients'. The following chapter explores how Paddington developed after MPU and some of the tensions and conflicts that its practice produced.

# CHAPTER FIVE

# Paddington Breakdown

During the protests many of the staff at Paddington had developed wider interests in bringing together an understanding of both the personal, political and institutional context. However, the political potential that had been opened up by the protest, and by the development of the MPU, was increasingly difficult to sustain. By the mid-1970s, the prevailing economic and political climate had shifted and counter-cultural struggles, which had helped to nourish the events at Paddington, had declined. The elation following the protests had died down and Paddington was left with some of its radical elements but lacking a wider social context in which to pursue radical ideas and aspirations, other than through psychoanalysis. The interests of politicised patients and the radical ideology of Paddington had coincided for a brief moment in their desire to challenge an individual 'illness' model. However, this shared vision was tested to its limits when differences became apparent between patients' demands and the particular psychotherapeutic enquiry insisted upon by the staff.

A series of official inquiries had alerted the public to the neglect, corruption and mistreatment in several large British psychiatric hospitals during the 1970s (Martin 1984). While the complainants or 'whistle-blowers' who initiated these were frequently marginalised members of staff such as students, part-time workers, assistants and orderlies (many of whom were also women), very few were patients themselves. By 1976, four years after patients had united with staff to save Paddington, a number of patients complained about the treatment and conditions at the day hospital and this led to two official inquiries and ultimately, by 1979 the day hospital closed. This chapter reviews the events that led to this situation.

This period in the life of the day hospital has been described as the 'Paddington events' (Millard 1985) or the 'Paddington disaster' (Sandison 1982) and has been analysed most memorably in Claire Baron's *Asylum to Anarchy* (1987). Commentaries about Paddington were littered throughout the therapeutic community literature of the time (Baron 1984b, 1985; Crocket 1985;

Crozier 1979; Ellison 1976; Goodburn 1986; Hinshelwood 1977; Millard 1985) and in the profession of group analysis (Ahlin 1981; Cooklin 1981; Kennard 1982; Kreeger 1981; Lemlij *et al.* 1982; Roberts 1982; Sandison 1982; Whiteley 1982, 1988). Accounts about the Paddington events were also written up in a number of unpublished papers (Crocket 1978; Goodburn 1977; Hall 1979; Lemlij *et al.* 1979) and the dispute gained local and national news coverage. Numerous debates developed after the demise of Paddington and these even included philosophical reflections regarding the nature of truth, the relationship between social and psychological ontology and epistemology (Millard 1985).

First, we need to know why Paddington developed in the way that it did. I aim to demonstrate that although this development may have contributed to its ultimate crisis and breakdown, there were some good reasons for the particular practice that was developed at Paddington, which have been lost in subsequent accounts. We will also see how staff responded to the challenges presented to them and the ideas and influences they drew upon to do so, specifically describing the influence of Henry Ezriel's psychoanalysis. Finally, we see how, despite good intentions, Paddington made insufficient attempts to understand how wider social determinants impacted on the community – factors that they were ill-equipped to deal with through relying on psychoanalysis alone.

## Emerging philosophy of practice at Paddington

During the period of protest Paddington was seen as an exciting and beneficial place by patients and workers. Referral rates were high, as was patient attendance at the various groups and meetings in the community. The tendency of numbers of referrals and attendees to rise during a public campaign has been documented elsewhere (Robinson 1994); however, as time elapsed, patients started to express their disillusionment through generally diminished attendance (Goodburn 1986). Events at Paddington after the protest both echoed changes that were occurring nationally and also expressed the patient and staff experience of political action and the difficulties of developing and sustaining a radical practice. In a national context, interest in TCs generally began to decline. In part this was because policies of 'community care', spurred on by critiques of traditional mental hospitals, fiscal constraints and the growing influence of the pharmaceutical industry, meant that acute psychiatry and short-stay, brief medicalised interventions became the norm. Low attendance and declining referrals to TCs reinforced a belief that they were under-used and therefore often recommended for closure (Hall 1979).

In the earlier 1970s there had been a number of flourishing alternative, often patient-run, independent initiatives in which dissatisfied patients could take refuge. However, alongside other counter-cultural projects, these also started to decline. By 1974 patients not only were less likely to be referred, but those who did attend also stopped attending the official small and large groups. These groups were part of the day hospital programme and are seen as essential to the therapeutic community model, yet increasing disillusionment and the impact of a generally declining radicalism, resulted in patients choosing to 'opt out'. This was expressed by patients beginning to meet as an informal group in the canteen (Goodburn 1986). While Goodburn had been critical of the TC model in that it provided an unnecessarily rigid structure to patients' lives, the core concept of the TC that the whole community should be involved in decision-making was still seen as crucial to the running of the day hospital.

However, the prevailing situation presented the Paddington staff with a dilemma. They attempted to manage this dilemma in line with their own libertarian (and psychoanalytically informed) philosophy. Despite the informal meetings in the canteen, the greatest attendance and interaction occurred during the middle of the day in the large group and this was a consistent remnant of the original day hospital programme. Staff used this group, which every community member was welcome to attend, to initiate a collective discussion of the ongoing situation. While other activities and groups (such as small groups) still continued around this event, the large group effectively acted as the main event of the community day and the major forum for discussion and psychotherapy in the day hospital. During this period Paddington differed from other TCs in that it combined these two functions. Most TCs have a regular community meeting at which decisions are made regarding the functioning of the whole community, patient committee meetings, a large psychotherapy group and other therapy groups and activities. At Paddington during this time there was no specific and separate decision-making forum.

At the same time, many of the other initiatives that looked to the wider community gradually declined. For example, the patients' commune, which had been so lauded in the early 1970s, gradually petered out and was no longer a focus of energy or development (Hall 1979). Such activities had been one of the hallmarks of the day hospital, yet the decline of wider social struggles seemed to result in a shift in emphasis within Paddington from outward looking, and politically inspired, activity to a more psychoanalytic focus on the 'large group' as an agent of change.

For staff this response was legitimate in that it did not impose artificial rules and regulations, which they felt could only serve to reproduce wider social configurations and structures (Goodburn 1976; Reder 1976). Rather than insisting that patients attend groups or institute any specific rules of attendance or discharge, patients could continue to attend but would be required to take part in an ongoing discussion of the individual and collective dynamics of the community. Their intention was to try and develop a situation in which there was ongoing, mutual and open enquiry.

This practice became central to the emerging identity of the day hospital in the aftermath of the protest. For example, in the early years of the Association of Therapeutic Communities (ATC), annual conferences were held at different individual TCs and the 'host' community would present something of their practice and ideology for discussion. The conference was held at Paddington in 1975, during which time there were lively debates in the ATC concerning the structure and organisation of TCs and the ATC. The ATC bulletin contained criticism that other ATC conferences had been over-structured, but this time the conference was centred on a highly unstructured large group, in ways that represented Paddington philosophy. Although this set up was confusing and bewildering for many participants, following the conference some argued that it had surpassed the usual 'stultifying dialogue between host institution and visitors' and had forced the Association to look at itself and develop a theme for the next conference (Bott 1975, p.20). Goodburn raised the question of what was the most appropriate social system for an institution devoted to psychotherapy. This promoted discussion and general consensus that the identity of the community must continually be examined, which is the task of the whole community.

During this period the day hospital's opening hours between 9am and 5pm provided the boundary within which behaviour and emotions could be expressed, understood and challenged. An 'open door' policy operated whereby patients could self-refer and self-determine their attendance so it wasn't reliant on a lengthy 'selection' process. Many of the usual psychodynamic understandings were applied, for example, individuals' presence (and/or absence) was open for comment and interpretation. Traditional psychiatric assessments were avoided in favour of attempting to see how patients actually functioned in the community, such that patients could forge, as far as possible, their own unmediated relationship to the institution (Goodburn 1976).

Each individual was viewed as contributing to the formation of a 'common group theme' or a 'dominant anxiety of the day'. This theme could be collectively adjusted and modified in the community. As Goodburn (2000) reflected, leadership was viewed as shifting along with group dynamics:

The unspoken rule would be the object, the task that we are united here to undertake is one of enquiry... The person who seems to be illuminating that enquiry at that moment in time is the leader of that enquiry, as it were... If you could look at how the work would be orientated at any moment in time, and how the primary task might hope to be defined, it would be by the initiation of whoever it was who brought in the theme that seemed to catch on.

This approach was viewed as a process of mutual research into the intra-psychic, interpersonal and institutional obstacles to greater mutuality, freedom and growth. In this way it could be seen as expanding Tom Main's notion of an open ongoing 'culture of enquiry' (Main 1983; Norton 1996). All patients and staff were viewed as contributing both to the formation of common themes and to their understanding and interpretation. Therefore, it was important that staff and patients shared access to information so they could contribute on a more equal basis. Thus staff encouraged patients to attend all necessary meetings in the day hospital and shared information with patients. For example, Goodburn regularly copied his correspondence to staff and patients and exclusive staff-only meetings were discouraged. This had been reported elsewhere in TCs, for example Crozier (1979) describes such an approach in response to patients' requests at Marlborough Day Hospital.

It is clear that Paddington remained a radical force in the development of TC practice in this period. Their insistence on the large group as the centre of community decision-making kept the concept of social action on the TC agenda even in a period of relative political acquiescence. The staff did not have a prescriptive model but they were responding in practice to a changing context. In this period they drew heavily on the ideas of Henry Ezriel, which seemed to offer a way of using psychoanalytic theory that did not deny the importance of wider social structures. They regularly attended group sessions with Ezriel outside the day hospital and his teaching played an extremely important part in the development of psychotherapy at Paddington. These ideas seemed to offer a way to hold on to the radical elements of the past while moving forward their therapeutic practice. However, despite these egalitarian premises, the practice at Paddington fell short of the ideal and many central ideas, such as those of Ezriel, were not brought to, or developed in collaboration with, the patient group. The way in which staff used his ideas in the development of Paddington, and the limitations of their application, is given more detailed attention in the next section.

# The influence of Ezriel, psychoanalysis and interpretation

Henry Ezriel was not known as a radical but his ideas had some influence in psychodynamic group therapies and group analysis and were applied in the potentially radical context of the day hospital. Ezriel had outlined the importance of full and totalising interpretations of group and individual phenomena in group psychotherapies (1950, 1952, 1959). At Paddington the absence of anything but the bare minimum of structure and leadership was seen as facilitating a greater understanding of the prevailing group and individual 'desired and avoided relationships'. One of Ezriel's premises was that externally imposed rules were often used to satisfy needs that then cannot be understood. Therefore, he maintained that it is best to leave the patient free from rules and regulations (1950). In becoming more aware of what patients avoided, and what they demanded to stand in its place, it was hoped that patients could become aware of, and move towards, the social relations they desired, but also feared.

The potentially radical, yet paradoxical, elements of the application of this approach were its refusal to treat community members as 'ill' and its adherence to psychoanalytic orthodoxy. This approach maintained that support, palliatives and reassurance would only prolong a person's difficulties, making life a little easier but not facilitating greater change and growth, either individually or in terms of challenging prevailing social structures. This model attempted to adhere to a more radical psychoanalytic vision (Jacoby 1975). Propping up defences with psychological and social crutches was viewed as being akin to a liberal reformist approach that stopped short of radical transformation. This transformation was viewed as being the ability of individuals, in their thoughts and action, to begin to try out and move towards the kinds of social relations that they genuinely desired in the world. Ultimately the rather ambitious goal of the staff was to help enable individuals to begin to take charge of their world and shape it as they saw fit.

One of the ways in which Ezriel's more conventional psychoanalytic views were applied to a more radicalised agenda and expectations at Paddington was the use of the psychoanalytic notion of transference to an institutional context. Thus Goodburn wrote and circulated an unpublished paper about the theory of practice of Paddington entitled 'Transference to the Institution' (1976). While there has been some more recent discussion about 'institutional transference' in group psychotherapies such as Tosquelle's movement of 'institutional psychotherapy' (Hochmann 1985), and Nitzgen's attempt at understanding of institutional transference in relation to analytic training institutes (1999), such notions are rarely used in TC (or group analytic) practices even today. For example, Blackwell (2000) recently urged group analysts to (re)consider the impact of hierarchical structures and institutions on the content of communication and individuality.

Goodburn's paper pointed out that the NHS and other wider social and institutional structures are frequently forgotten in traditional psychotherapies. The practice at Paddington was intended to rectify this by ensuring that this wider dimension was included in understanding the group and individual dynamics in the community. The 'institution' was conceived as being understood through what Ezriel called a 'three-part interpretation' (1950, 1952, 1959). Ezriel formulated the idea that patients had an unconscious fantasy regarding an imagined catastrophe that would happen if they dared to move out of their current accepted position or role in their social world. The institution was seen as the focus of patients' 'required' needs/relationship, which were viewed as a compromise between a wished for/desired relationship (the 'avoided relationship') and an accompanying fear of the *consequences* of entering into this desired relationship (the 'catastrophic' relationship). This fantasy must be fearful enough to justify the defensive formation of a 're-quired' relationship. This required relationship was conceived in terms of patients' demands for 'external' palliative solutions to difficulties such as medication and medical certificates which merely confirmed that they were 'ill' and ultimately kept them stuck within the required relationship or position.

A classic 'required' relationship, accepted by many group psychotherapists from Wilfred Bion onwards is the (often unconscious) demand for leadership that is projected into the therapist and/or staff team (Bion 1961). At Paddington this was seen to reflect wider authoritative or authoritarian social relations and configurations such as parents, employers, teachers and other 'experts'. We can see how these ideas converged with the role of Paddington in challenging the medical model and associated relationships expected within this, such as a reliance on medical expertise, diagnosis and treatment. The adoption of a sick role was thus viewed as a conservative force inhibiting social change, which could otherwise become a focus of dissatisfaction and conflict (Waitzkin and Waterman 1974). Staff felt that such demands both reproduced and reinforced prevailing ideas of 'mental illness' as well as bolstered and colluded with patients' own internalised restraints and lack of agency. We saw in previous chapters how Goodburn viewed signing patients' medical certificates as tantamount to invalidating individuals and confirming their role as passive patients.

Central to Ezriel's teaching was that staff could either meet patients' required relationships or they could facilitate an open enough environment through which to continue to analyse and challenge them with other people. Once the required relationship was met it was postulated that the emotional impetus for change had been subsumed and the accompanying frustration and tension had alleviated, at least for the time being. This meant that the issue or demand could no longer be explored until it was expressed again. Similar ideas are often used in psychoanalytically informed practices where facilitating patients' anger and frustration at not having certain needs met in therapy is thought to be an important avenue into a greater awareness, understanding and expression of unconscious feelings and motivations.

This idea was dramatically demonstrated in an example given by Goodburn (2000) of an event that occurred earlier in his career and that clearly influenced his ideas in this direction. Goodburn recalled being consulted by a woman patient who had a history of terrible abuse and who felt continually oppressed and victimised. She lived in terrible conditions and her presenting request (her 'required' relationship) was that she needed a new flat and basically felt that she would be all right if she had somewhere decent to live. However, when a well-intentioned social worker got involved and got her the flat she wanted, shortly afterwards she killed herself. For Goodburn this highlighted the difficulty with responding to symptomatic complaints that may mask more fundamental problems. Goodburn reflected that she had been able to live by her sense of being victimised and oppressed as a defence against unexpressed or unrecognised rage and anger. When this was interrupted, by giving her what she seemingly wanted, she turned her anger onto herself.

The approach developed at Paddington was, therefore, an attempt to facilitate in patients a greater awareness, and expression, of the realities of past and present situations and injustices. Complying with patients' material requests was seen as stopping the emergence of an awareness of the emotional impact of the real deprivation suffered, which these requests might 'represent'. Therefore, many of the support structures and assistance that patients expected and demanded were gradually questioned as part of an ongoing process that developed at Paddington. It was this particular reasoning and application of theory that caused the most difficult, enduring and ultimate conflict at Paddington, and later in this chapter I will describe how patients reacted to this situation. In the meantime, however, the next section explores some specific examples of how, despite their radical impetus and rationale, the way in which these ideas were put into practice was often insufficiently communicated and sometimes clumsy. Moreover, despite their best intentions, the team at Paddington did not sufficiently integrate an understanding of the wider social context into their practice.

## The missing dimension?

As mentioned earlier, despite attempts to see Paddington as part of a wider institutional context, the project often failed sufficiently to deal with the impact of wider social dynamics both inside and outside Paddington. Moreover, the project had a number of effects that were not adequately addressed and which may have contributed to its crisis and decline. First, an important issue that was not addressed, neither at Paddington nor in any subsequent accounts, was the importance of gender dynamics. The ability of Paddington to work with disaffected men, who were not ordinarily accessing psychiatric nor psychotherapeutic services, reversed the usual predominance of women clients in services and was seen as part of its uniqueness and importance. However, a gradual decline in the numbers of women patients attending the day hospital should have been a cause for concern (Plunket *et al.* 1976). By 1976, there were very few women patients reported as attending (Baron 1987; Crocket 1978). A number of examples were given about women patients in written publications about Paddington – for example, Baron described instances where she feels women patients were treated poorly, and her analysis also makes much of the position of the (male) consultant and the effects of his hidden, yet abusive authority. However, in none of the numerous commentaries and analyses of the demise of Paddington have these been explored specifically in terms of the politics of social and gendered relational dynamics.

Paddington can be viewed as reflecting traditional gender structures in having a male consultant and a male chair of the Paddington Centre and Day Hospital, alongside predominantly women administration workers, cleaners and cooks. Indeed, many of Goodburn's so-called 'followers' were women (Baron 1984a, 1987). Other examples outlined below also draw attention to wider institutional dynamics, whereby socially ascribed positions 'outside', or on the margins of, Paddington were gendered and racialised. Thus, for example, institutionally racialised groups occupied the space of the excluded – badly paid and poorly treated at Paddington, both as cooks and cleaners. Such positions unfortunately reflect wider institutional racialised dynamics which are all too common in professional practices.

Staff made two key decisions during this period which arose from the application of the theoretical framework discussed above. A more detailed exploration of these decisions, both the radical impulse behind them and their effects, highlights the limitations of Paddington in making sense of the wider social and institutional context. Decisions such as these were made as a result of an uncomfortable fit between the desire to challenge dominant structures of oppression and marginalisation and the (over) use of psychoanalytic ideas to inform practice.

The context in which these decisions were taken was as follows. After the successful protest in 1971 it had been anticipated that the feared transfer to St Mary's might happen through the back door with the pending administrative reorganisation and structural changes that would occur throughout the NHS in 1974. However, by 1974 the impetus of the protest had receded and awareness of this change, and its potential impact, had effectively ceased. Having successfully fought the transfer, the new reorganisation in 1974 resulted in a change of management of the day hospital and gave increased power to consultants. Goodburn recalled how these changes went ahead effectively unnoticed, partly due to a lack of any clearly visible change in management or administration. However, they did result in him, as the consultant, being asked to take decisions that had previously been made by the wider administration.

Soon after these administrative changes, the hospital administrators asked Goodburn what he wanted to do about the day hospital cleaner who had just left. Goodburn was not used to being asked to make such decisions. However, he was disillusioned with the degree to which patients were taking responsibility for their behaviour in the day hospital and the staff team were increasingly questioning the need for material provisions in the day hospital anyway (as they were seen as interfering with collective understanding). Therefore, he decided not to replace the cleaner without consulting the rest of the community. Given that the day hospital was getting particularly untidy, it was an attempt to contain the situation within the community and ensure that patients and staff took more responsibility for cleaning the day hospital themselves. The thinking behind this decision was, in many ways, well intentioned and multi-layered, since the decision was also intended to challenge the patients' treatment of a socially marginalised cleaner. The cleaner was a disabled south-east Asian woman who Goodburn felt was disrespected by patients who, for example, dropped cigarette butts on the floor and left them for her to clean up.

However, the thinking behind this decision was not well communicated within the community as a whole. Furthermore, although it had significant implications in terms of opening up opportunities to increase the potential autonomy and decision-making capacity of the community as a whole, this potential was lost. In retrospect, not only did Goodburn later regard his unilateral decision as a 'foolish and gross mistake', he also reflected that it indicated more generally that everyone at Paddington (himself, the staff and the patients) lacked sufficient collective understanding of how outside institutional factors impacted on the community.

The lack of a cleaner was an issue that patients later referred to in their official complaints in 1976. Furthermore, this decision set the context for the second important decision that was made in the day hospital which resulted in a proposal to withdraw meals and travel fares. It was current practice at Paddington (and other NHS facilities) at this time that patients attending Paddington who received social security payments could receive a free meal and have their travel costs reimbursed. Following continued discussions about material provisions in the day hospital, some of the staff group, unbeknownst to the others and perhaps taking a lead from the consultant's earlier decision, issued a letter proposing the withdrawal of lunches and travel allowances to the patient group. (In fact, as a result of consequent complaints and the impending inquiry, this proposal was never actually implemented.)

Rather than group members (staff and patients) collectively deciding how and what they would do about food – perhaps preparing and cooking together (as regularly happens in TCs now) – food was prepared outside the boundaries of the day hospital, brought in and served. The specific idea of withdrawing certain provisions was intended as a positive move towards dealing with difficulties arising from the open-door policy. For example, it was designed to help ensure those attending the day hospital did so in order to engage in a psychotherapeutic project, rather than to receive other 'benefits'. In this decision, as well as in the other key decision about the cleaner, racial and gender dynamics were apparent, but again the implications of these were not fully explored by staff (or patients) in the community. For example, the two cooks who had originally been employed at Paddington were two black women from St Lucia. However, due to changes beyond the scope of the day hospital, the food was no longer prepared on the premises, so they were effectively demoted just to serving pre-prepared food (Goodburn 1986). Again this example illustrates how the boundaries of decision-making between the day hospital, the rest of the centre and the wider administration became increasingly unclear (Crocket 1978).

In TCs generally the negotiation and collective resolution of such tasks is frequently seen as being integral to therapy, as well as a constant source of difficulty. Therefore, in many ways both decisions could have moved the day hospital more in line with a therapeutic community model, ensuring that the community itself had sufficient autonomy to think about and collectively resolve ongoing practical living arrangements rather than leaving them to be provided for elsewhere.

One of the key difficulties about Paddington was that the wider social network within which the day hospital was situated was unsuitable for a therapeutic community attempting to work in such an open and permissive way

(Crocket 1978). While this seems crucial in understanding some of the problems which beset Paddington, it has rarely figured in many subsequent critiques of Paddington. In his unpublished paper about Paddington, Crocket maintained that a TC needs to be able to control its own boundaries, selection of staff, time commitments and space, which Paddington was unable to do. He argued that Paddington did not have enough freedom of action to respond to the needs of its patients in its own way. For example, patients and staff had insufficient autonomy to be able to develop their own self-defined and libertarian guidelines, structures and support mechanisms.

The development of the approach at Paddington can be seen, in part, as encompassing various attempts to deal with these boundary problems permissively. For example, the lack of structure, the extension of the 'large group' to cover the whole day and delineating membership of the community as anyone who attended during the opening hours were all attempts to create a flexible boundary for practicing an open therapeutic enquiry within a larger institutional NHS setting. However, lack of control over the wider structures of power and decision-making made the maintenance of ongoing, open enquiry that was free from 'interference' impossible.

Moreover, these two decisions also highlighted a number of other key tensions and, in particular, exposed discrepancies between the official ideology of the day hospital and the actual power base within the community. It is precisely these discrepancies that illustrate the difficulties in TCs as a whole. Specifically, these decisions exposed the problem of relying upon a psychoanalytic framework, which too readily results in other considerations being marginalised. As Goodburn (2000) reflected:

> [Psychoanalysis] obviously wasn't sufficient to deal with that situation. And it was quite clear that, you know, the situation itself was determined by a whole lot of factors that I really hadn't taken on board…it was essentially what was outside the boundary, and how did that influence and determine what was going on in Paddington.

The critique that TCs, psychoanalysis and psychotherapy in general lack an appropriate socio-cultural dimension is not new (Blackwell 2000). In a lengthy interview with two key protagonists of the Paddington approach we discussed a number of examples in which this 'external dimension' was 'missed'. Goodburn reflected on what kinds of questions would be commensurate with such an approach:

> Within what context is this taking place? What are the relevant aspects of that context at any moment in time? I mean there are always a thousand and

> one clues. Well, I don't think we were picking them up, that's the problem... I suppose in Paddington...all sorts of things would have come on the agenda. What does the State do? What does government do? Who really governs? Where's democracy? What's democracy?... A thousand and one different questions would have been available to study, once, you know, the doors had been left open... But maybe [they] weren't... It could be the sort of things you were talking about, you know, of inadequate housing, food, funding... Which leads you straight on to well, you know, what is the nature of the state, the Welfare State, the provisions, where do these funds come from, how are they to be distributed to – who's deserving of them, etc.

These two decisions were not just 'mistakes' but symbolised a more fundamental problem beyond that of just 'missing' certain issues or not 'picking them up' sufficiently. Even if the decisions had not been made the day hospital would still have had to attend to ongoing difficulties relating to the boundary between itself and the world outside the day hospital. Unfortunately, when brought face to face with the importance of a third (outside/external world) dimension, staff effectively denied or ignored this, rather than attempting to understand or even challenge it.

In many ways, patients' complaints, as discussed below, could actually be viewed as another attempt to engage with this 'external dimension'. In reaching out to wider (external) structures of power – both through the content and the means of the complaint – patients, in effect, highlighted this missing dimension.

> In that case you could look upon the complaints, which were to an external body... Almost as an attempt to test out – extend – that boundary in order to get things going elsewhere, because the Ezrielian type of interpretation did not refer to the external dimension. ... That would postulate a very hypothetical hypothesis... That if one had given a three-part interpretation with that dimension included, then one could have continued to function perhaps...so then we start examining the society as part of the task...I think that it was remiss that that dimension was subsequently lost after the protest. (Goodburn 2000)

However, the idea that a 'fuller' or more complete interpretation would have overcome these conflicts and avoided the subsequent crisis overlooks the complex interplay of dynamics and tensions that connect the outside and inside of TCs. Thus while the two decisions drew attention to wider institutional structures and changes that lay outside the remit of the community, they also highlighted a number of issues relating to an awareness of, and subsequent action about, complex socially determined dynamics within the community. Unfortunately, and unwittingly, these decisions did not address the prevailing inter-relational dynamics and perhaps only served to sideline them. Whether or not the decisions should be considered 'mistakes' in retrospect, they did highlight and challenge the idea of patients' self-determination in the day hospital.

## Patients' complaints and the closure of Paddington

While the philosophy developed at Paddington advocated shared decision-making, this was obviously difficult when staff held particularly strong beliefs regarding the necessity for certain types of help and not others. As visitors from the patient group at the neighbouring Malborough Day Hospital pointed out, the whole community at Paddington did not have input into the overall philosophy of Paddington (Plunket *et al.* 1976). Paddington lacked an explicit decision-making forum through which this philosophy could be developed and modified with the patients. In addition, a failure by the staff to communicate to patients discrepancies between the ideology of shared decision-making and the notion of a shared psychoanalytic enquiry resulted in considerable patient unrest and confusion.

In the year leading up to their official complaint in 1976, patients made a number of informal complaints. In particular, many patients felt that the provision of material benefits was essential to their welfare and did not appreciate the ways in which these were questioned in the name of greater psychological awareness and understanding. It is usual practice in TCs for patients' informal complaints and grievances to be referred back to the whole community so that a deeper understanding of the issue can be developed as part of the therapeutic community process. This was no different at Paddington. However, patients felt that this effectively aborted their legitimate grievances, making complaining a futile exercise. More specifically, patients felt their complaints were pathologised as they were often viewed as attempts to satisfy their 'required' relationships and therefore not taken seriously. This attempt to develop a deeper understanding of their motivations for certain demands often resulted in interpretations which left patients feeling ridiculed by staff if they complained.

While the Paddington philosophy of 'transference to the institution' may have been important in trying to keep the relationship between patients and their institutional context under critique, one participant reflected that:

> In a sense it's almost the other way round. I think that having recognised that, that covertly what Paddington did was foster it and behave as though what the patients were going to do is to become dependent on the institution or something like that, and then be mocked for that. (Anon 2000)

The final straw came in January 1976 when patients received the letter proposing to stop the provision of meals and travel reimbursements. As Baron has outlined, this 'concrete' decision gave patients the opportunity to challenge the locus of power and authority in the day hospital itself. In a fascinating account showing insight into patients growing resistance and collective organisation, Baron (1987) suggests that it was because the decision touched patients in more practical and material terms that this led to an appeal to the authorities. She argues that when the interpretations and questioning of assistance expanded from medical certificates and medication to more immediate practical and material provisions in the day hospital such as travel fares and meals, patients' opposition became more unified and focused. This concrete proposal gave patients a focus for their grievances and dissatisfaction and enabled them to respond as a coherent group, and this kick started more collectivised action.

Approximately half the group of patients who regularly attended the day hospital signed an official letter of complaint asking for the conditions at Paddington to be reviewed. They sent this letter to the District Health Administrator, the Department of Health and Social Security, the Professional Staff Committee of the Paddington Centre and Goodburn. Patients also contacted the local and national media; perhaps a strategy carried over from the protest and the initial MPU meetings. Most, but not all, of these patients also signed a subsequent letter of complaint calling for an immediate inspection of the day hospital and an inquiry.

The complaints focused on a number of issues. Patients protested about the extent to which they were actually involved in decision-making in the day hospital and, in particular, wanted specific patient representation at meetings where decisions were made, especially about provisions and assistance. They expressed concern about the over-reliance on psychoanalytic interpretation at the expense of support for their more immediate social problems. The interpretations they received in response to their complaints led many to feel that they were not treated respectfully but with 'mockery and derision':

> We as patients are attending the Paddington Hospital for treatment and not to be treated with ridicule not indeed to be the guinea pigs in some bizarre experiment that appears to be going on. (Letter signed 'the day patients', reprinted in KCWAHA 1976)

Baron (1987) recalled how patients developed their own alternative views of their motivation for attending the day hospital – for example, as a social club; a haven from loneliness; or a place to get a meal and companionship. In addition, patients often resisted interpretations by drawing upon other culturally circulating narratives. For example, they compared the day hospital to the popular book and film *One Flew over the Cuckoo's Nest* and referred to 'cuckoo games' played out by staff (Baron 1984a).

In a social context where 'sickness' is required in order to gain various forms of social assistance and benefits, Paddington seemed like a conservative libertarianism rather than the development of a greater collectivisation of mental health care (Sedgwick 1982). Unless wider practices of social welfare, exclusion and the medical model are challenged on a broader scale, the libertarianism promoted at Paddington is dangerously close to the New Right/New Labour ideological consensus of individualism, responsibility and citizenship. This consensus utilises notions of the 'Nanny State' and 'state dependency' which are used to justify attacks on welfare provision. In reflecting on being a patient at Paddington, Lawson (1999) highlighted the importance of material assistance, which he felt was (and is) lacking in mental health services generally:

> At grassroots level you got your dinner there! And these basic things are really important... The more mental health professionalism one receives the further away one gets from one's actual dinner!

A number of disaffected patients had already left Paddington after becoming dissatisfied and disillusioned with the alternative psychiatry offered, which some felt amounted to a 'therapeutic bullying'. Some more politicised patients became more involved in alternative patient-run initiatives such as the MPU and People Not Psychiatry, where they found more support, solidarity and assistance. Some did both. For example, Eric Irwin, one of the key founder members of the MPU, still attended Paddington, as well as being active in the patients' movement and anti-psychiatry. Despite their criticisms many of the patients felt there was still something to be gained from its practice and wanted more influence over its direction.

An official inquiry was subsequently initiated into Paddington. This found 'ample evidence' to support the patients' complaints and made a list of recommendations with which the day hospital should comply. However, some staff and patients were keen to continue their way of working and Goodburn decided to offer two different types of therapy. One type would comply with the inquiry's recommendations and the other would continue to try to develop an open psychoanalytic enquiry without interference or material provisions. Patients could choose which therapy they wanted to join and thus patients who complained could have their demands satisfied by attending the other sessions. While seeming to be a reasonable suggestion offering a unique opportunity to evaluate and compare the two approaches, his proposal did not satisfy the Area Health Authority who demanded that all the recommendations had to be met for all patients.

In November 1976, when Goodburn refused to comply with these recommendations, he was suspended. This resulted in a second inquiry, which was a more serious and protracted legal disciplinary process concentrating on the conduct of Goodburn himself, and eventually led to the recommendation that he be dismissed for unprofessional or 'wrong' practice, but not malpractice (Baron 1984a). This meant that although the health authority no longer wished to employ him he was not struck off the professional register. In effect, he could no longer work as a consultant in the NHS and, if he continued working in the NHS, he would have been demoted to a registrar position. In fact, Goodburn no longer worked in the NHS or in the therapeutic community field after Paddington. Following a number of productive visits to Russia and developing his interest in Marxist psychologists such as Lev Vygotsky and Alexander Luria, he went on to develop a small independent therapy practice well into his sixties and until his sudden death in 2001 (Spandler 2001).

Meanwhile, a number of patients struggled to be involved in developing the future of Paddington and this is evident in notes from minutes of patients' meetings during this time. Most of the 'hard core' of the twelve patients who signed the complaint continued to attend the day hospital (Plunket et al. 1976, p.11). Although some patients gave evidence that was to condemn Paddington, those who presided over the ultimate decision regarding the fate of Paddington didn't actually invite or encourage them to become actively involved in changing it, or for that matter consult about whether it should be closed. Patients had to fight to even get hold of copies of the inquiry report as they were only permitted to see the summary (Baron 1987). Patients managed to get hold of the report anyway, by setting off the fire alarm in the day hospital and retrieving a copy when people left the building (Baron 1987). A patients' spokesperson commented that it had been a 'confused and unsatisfactory position and many of us cannot understand why the report from the committee of inquiry has been kept secret. We can only hope that the new steps and inquiry will clear the air.' (Paddington Mercury 1976b, p.36).

Although the second inquiry only recommended Goodburn's dismissal, the Executive Committee of the Paddington Centre wanted to disassociate itself from its bad reputation and proposed the day hospital be closed down.

Under pressure to economise, the Area Health Authority capitalised on this proposal and called for the whole Paddington Centre (including the day hospital) to be closed down. They maintained that it 'would not be appropriate to allocate scarce resources to a facility of such limited scope and application in terms of services for the mentally ill generally' (report by Area Health Authority quoted in Baron 1984a, p.370).

Although patients certainly initiated the first inquiry into Paddington, the decision to close it clearly came from a higher authority. The earlier campaign to save Paddington embodied patients' refusal to play a passive patient role and wait for decisions to be made about its future. In this later crisis, by an ironic twist, they did have to wait for a higher authority to cast judgement on Paddington. Although Paddington was closed, the Paddington Centre for Psychotherapy survived, moving to new premises and remodelled as the Parkside Clinic which exists to this day, albeit significantly without a day hospital or therapeutic community.

Richard Crocket was appointed to take over as consultant on a temporary basis during Goodburn's suspension. Crocket was an important pioneer of the psychotherapeutic community approach and was the director of the Ingrebourne Centre therapeutic community at Hornchurch, in Essex (Crocket 1966). Although he tried to reinstitute a therapeutic community culture in the day hospital, demoralisation and splits that had developed in the staff team (some of whom tried to continue the work they had developed with Goodburn) made this a difficult prospect. To make matters worse, Paddington was becoming notorious and estranged from the Paddington Centre and the wider community. Furthermore, as we will see in Chapter Seven, the day hospital became increasingly pathologised. These factors, plus the wider political context being less conducive to therapeutic communities and particular libertarian initiatives such as Paddington, eventually resulted in Crocket having to run Paddington down.

Paddington finally closed its doors in 1979 and the subsequent long reign of a Conservative government meant collectivised approaches such as therapeutic communities in general faced further decline (Winship and Haigh 2000). Crocket tried to get social service's support for a day centre away from the hospital where he hoped the staff might be able to continue their work in a more favourable environment, but this proved impossible (Crocket 1978). In response to Baron's critique of Paddington he later argued:

> I hope that someday, somewhere, someone will be in a position to repeat what the Medical Director of the Paddington tried to do. The external and internal circumstances will have to be totally different. I have little doubt that this will happen. (Crocket 1985, p.113–4)

Despite many valid criticisms levelled at its practice, Paddington was a serious attempt at developing a context that was open enough to facilitate mutual understanding and enquiry, where patients could develop and organise their own structures with limited external constraints and structures. However, despite these good intentions, the approach gave rise to particular tensions and conflicts. It was not only the radical set up or a series of 'mistakes' that led to increasing conflict but an over-emphasis on psychoanalytic understandings at the expense of a consideration of wider social determinants and shared decision-making structures. In subsequent chapters I will explore how similar tensions figure in TC practices generally. In particular, in the next chapter I renew the ways in which these events have been constructed as a dominant narrative to describe the failure of radical TCs.

# CHAPTER SIX

# Asylum to Anarchy?

The previous chapters have presented three distinct periods in the life of Paddington Day Hospital. The first stage was viewed as a 'Victorious Protest' (Ward 1972), in which a TC threatened by closure was saved by a successful campaign. In the second period, a politicised patients group, the MPU, was forged from the earlier struggle and displayed the changed consciousness and organising skills that the protest had given them (Crossley 1999a). The final stage of the day hospital discussed here has usually been viewed as a story of radical failure and/or a cautionary tale highlighting the dangers of charismatic leadership and psychoanalytic imperialism. It has also been seen as indicating the inherent impossibility of the therapeutic community itself (Lemlij *et al.* 1982). Another less articulated reading of the events is a story of the triumph of a group of oppressed patients overthrowing a psychiatric, anti-psychiatric or psychoanalytic tyranny. Yet when we step back, and view Paddington as a whole, the complexity of the picture disrupts any attempt to provide a linear narrative of events. This chapter attempts to review the dominant accounts and analyses of the decline of Paddington.

## Asylum to anarchy

In trying to understand the decline of a radical therapeutic community, one particular narrative has gained dominance: one in which a radical and idealistic TC descends into disorganisation and failure. This narrative has resurfaced a number of times in the therapeutic community literature. Here, I examine some examples of this, particularly reviewing the work of Robert Hobson (1979) and Claire Baron (1987). Although the conclusions that could be drawn from Baron's analysis were the subject of much debate, her account still remains the most memorable and recounted version of events at Paddington and has left a lasting legacy. I also explore Hobson's narrative because although it was not written specifically about Paddington, it is often referred to in explaining crises which have beset TCs, and Paddington in particular (Kreeger 1981; Lemlij *et al.* 1979, 1982). Hobson's paper was originally circulated as an unpublished discussion paper in 1971 and later published in an edited collection on TCs (Hinshelwood and Manning 1979). Hobson himself was later to become a member of the official panel of Inquiry into Paddington, and this may have influenced his later article.

Despite coming from the different disciplines and perspectives of psychotherapy and sociology respectively, Hobson and Baron's accounts draw on a single powerful narrative, which I will refer to more generally (using the title of Baron's book) as *Asylum to Anarchy*. While Baron wrote what is primarily a sociological account of Paddington to provide a damning critique of the day hospital, drawing on Goffman's infamous critique of asylums (1961) and Foucault's ideas about technologies of power and knowledge (1971, 1977), Hobson drew more upon psychotherapeutic concepts. Hobson (1979) provided a model of what he called 'the messianic community' which utilised the narrative of decline, describing it as a process of 'idealisation to catastrophe'. He tells us a cautionary tale of the dangers of TCs succumbing to the problems of idealisation and becoming seemingly 'messianic', in what he provocatively termed the 'therapeutic community disease'. Although Baron doesn't explicitly use Hobson's model of the messianic community and only briefly mentions it (1987, p.75), she, too, draws upon a similar narrative.

In *Asylum to Anarchy* Baron describes how a radical experiment in mental health democracy and liberty, turned into anarchy, chaos and tyranny. She describes how a wayward medical director, 'Adrian' (Goodburn) encouraged his staff to abandon all rules and structures in a vain attempt at introducing greater democracy and freedom in the day hospital. She demonstrates how this left patients at the mercy of relentless and obscure psychoanalytic interpretation of their every motive and piece of behaviour.

While the recurrence of these narratives might appear to suggest that they are true, it is important to bear in mind that in working with any models or concepts we are not dealing directly with reality, but rather with instruments or lenses with or through which to read reality (Melucci 1995). These narratives 'work' not necessarily because they are 'true', but because their narratives are so deeply structured and heavily infused into Western culture and discourse (Parker 1997). The next section describes this dominant narrative in more detail and highlights both its usefulness and accuracy to the events at Paddington, as well as the omissions that can occur when such narratives are employed uncritically.

## Idealisation to catastrophe

In his essay 'The Messianic Community', Hobson (1979) described three stages a therapeutic community can move through: from idealisation to catastrophe. Hobson calls the first stage 'The coming of the messiah' where processes of idealisation are unleashed through the arrival of a new charismatic leader. The new leader is seen as representing 'the light of democracy' and attracting a committed following as well as fierce opposition from the establishment, including both real and perceived threats. In Hobson's scenario, the leader comes to represent both a saviour hero to some, and a dangerous revolutionary to others. During this period, Hobson argues, patients' symptoms may improve, strikingly, but only temporarily (p.234).

Hobson argued that the radical and democratic aims of charismatic newcomers can create unrealistically high expectations, and a deep confusion between a necessary 'ideal' and a problematic process of 'idealisation'. He argues that while an ideal is necessarily unattainable but involves hope and aspiration such an ideal can too easily, particularly in periods of heightened activity and expectation, become an 'idealisation'. Idealisation characterises a situation in which participants are unable to recognise the necessary failure of the ideal and results in a denial of anything that represents failure. If not recognised and challenged, these denied facts or 'reality' return, threatening disorganisation and disintegration.

It is generally agreed in most accounts of Paddington that there was a problem with idealisation, charismatic leadership and therapeutic omnipotence (Baron 1987; Crocket 1978; Kreeger 1981; Lemlij *et al.* 1979, 1982; Oakley 1989). According to this view, the euphoria of the protests and Goodburn's subsequent idealisation resulted in an unquestioning acceptance of his more wayward ideas and practices and this turned into an 'omnipotent charismatic analytic crusade', which lost touch with reality (Crocket 1978, p.29). Commentators have particularly focused on the earlier protests to defend Paddington as being central to this process:

> For the experiment which ended in crisis could not, I would argue, have been initiated, let alone taken root for as long as it did, if it had not been for the earlier crisis in the history of the Day Hospital when staff and patients together defended psychotherapy against more traditional psychiatric methods that were being bureaucratically imposed on them. (Baron 1987, p.24)

In this scenario, the protests brought to bear an idealisation of both psychotherapy and the bearer of these insights, the Medical Director (Goodburn), who inherited the position of 'saviour' or 'messiah'. In part this was seen to be generated by his activity in the successful campaign, which contributed to his growing attraction as a charismatic leader (Crocket 1978) as he 'earned his right to be separate' (Lemlij *et al.* 1982, p.5).

> The Medical Director's authority was developed from his role of saviour in the protest and was seen to symbolise the values that had been fought for. He was approvingly regarded as a radical because he emphasised the superiority of psychoanalytic knowledge, denied his and others' formal positions any special authority and, by abandoning all rules, declared that the day clinic should be run completely democratically. (Baron 1984a, p.96)

Baron argued that heightened politicisation and activism developed a sense of unity and solidarity amongst both staff and patients, which idealised the medical director and allowed him to usher in a new regime which overstepped the limits of therapeutic acceptability. He claims that the exclusive emphasis on the psyche of patients could take hold only when, through the polarisation of attitudes that developed during the protest, participants had come to idealise the psychoanalytic reality of the unconscious.

This tendency was seen to be tied up with the campaign, which viewed the day hospital approach as a radical alternative to mainstream psychiatry. In order to mount a defence of the day hospital, the case for its existence had to be (over) stated and a sharp dividing line drawn between what was offered at Paddington and 'psychiatry' in general. While this strategy was necessary and effective during the campaign, it also glossed over important similarities and complexities, both within 'traditional' psychiatry and the 'alternative' offered at the day hospital itself. The possibility of community psychotherapy within the NHS for patients usually deemed 'unsuitable' was worth fighting for, but perhaps raised unrealistic expectations of what was achievable. It was argued that this resulted in overstating the possibilities and applicability of psychotherapy, including its ability to withstand extremes of disturbance and its ability to treat every kind of patient (Baron 1987; Oakley 1989).

An indirect result of the protests was a belief that more conventional ideas accepted in most psychiatric institutions could be discarded, and this ushered in the possibility of the development and expansion of the Paddington's boundaries in relation to democratisation *and* psychotherapy. It was both of these two crucial elements that were highlighted and fought for during the campaign and that were extended in scope and practice after its success.

> Through this display of solidarity, an even more democratic style of participation developed in the Day Hospital and the emphasis upon therapeutic

treatment methods and democratic participation during this period of conflict…provided an advantageous climate for a further extension of the therapeutic community approach in the Day Hospital. (Baron 1984b, pp.158–9)

Thus Baron claimed that the protest 'precipitated', and provided a 'seedbed' for the later crisis as it had a 'radicalising effect on the day hospital and provided a fertile ground for so extreme an approach' (p.40). The gradual relaxation of rules and structures at Paddington was one of the important factors highlighted in accounts of Paddington's demise (Baron 1987; KCWAHA 1976; Lemlij *et al.* 1979). This was attributed, largely, to the success and camaraderie that developed during the protests (Baron 1984a).

The idea of a lack of structure could have appealed to people's sense of achievement after the successful campaign, where an eagerness to explore and experiment with new radical ideas contributed to a sense in which participants felt they were at the forefront of innovations. In particular, staff witnessed, and benefited from, the patients' ability to take on responsibilities during the campaign, and so relaxed the rules governing the day hospital, allowing patients to organise their own structures (Baron 1984a).

There are very few studies of the complex dynamics which are engendered during the process of mounting a protest or campaign in a TC. One exception is an account of a campaign to save the Cassel therapeutic community in the early 1990s (Robinson 1994). As at Paddington, this was also a highly public protest involving patients, the public and the media. Robinson discussed how, during the campaign, divisions within the TC were no longer acknowledged and projected outside. That tendency had resulted from a need to project a highly successful image of the Cassel to the outside world, even though the work was not, in fact, always so successful:

> With the threat of closure, all of the powerful destructive feelings that patients bring with them and hopefully resolve were suddenly banished. This was the single most destructive aspect that threat of closure brought… We ceased being able to look at the interpersonal dynamics now having a common external enemy on which we could project all our hostile conflicts. Patients and staff became one solid group defending 'our precious Cassel' from outside attack… This created a great sense of togetherness. (Robinson 1994, p.80)

The necessary reaction to preserve the therapeutic community meant that the ongoing difficulties inherent in developing a radical practice were suspended, or put on hold, only to resurface later. The rush for consensus and a degree of solidarity necessary to mount a successful campaign can result in the suppression of difference and debate. These difficulties might be indicative of a wider problem in some protest movements and organisations which are marked by a lack of reflective practice, not so much about the actual decisions made, but about how they are made (Rowbotham, Segal and Wainwright 1980).

The crisis at Paddington was later described as 'a dream betrayed', and a 'story of calamitous disappointment set within a context of the highest expectations' (Oakley 1989, p.110). It is clear that the day hospital had established a radical reputation for itself, partly as a result of the protests. The campaign certainly raised expectations regarding the possibility of an alternative that could offer something more humane and democratic than conventional psychiatry. Paddington experienced an initial surge in admissions after the protest (Goodburn 1986) and attracted intelligent patients wanting to experience more democratic treatment methods (Baron 1987). An account by a Paddington patient highlighted the expectations and hope he had about Paddington, which had come to his attention after seeing the film *Family Life*:

> After all, the Paddington Day Clinic, which only a few months before had won a militant campaign to stay open, was reputed to be the most progressive National Health centre for neurosis in the whole country… If anyone could help me, it was they. (Small undated, p.6)

However, once Paddington emerged intact from the external threat, it faced the arduous task of meeting these expectations and some patients soon became disillusioned. It has often been commented that groups regress when faced with such difficult tasks and the need to assess their aims, feasibility and resources (Sturdy 1987).

In Hobson's second stage, the 'enlightenment', the above processes are recognised intellectually but this recognition only serves to reinforce the idealistic and messianic fantasy, so that 'now we know ourselves' (1979, p.234). Hobson argued that this can result in an abundance of pretentious and frequently dogmatic formulations. Baron's account is littered with possible examples of these formulations at Paddington. Thus she refers to the rather smug and even mocking attitude of the staff at Paddington, assuming that they 'knew' the underlying unconscious motivations of patients' (and workers') behaviour. Indeed, the use of Ezriel's notion of a 'correct' and total interpretation may itself have been an indication of these processes in action. Moreover, this tendency to provide intellectualised interpretations was one of patients' objections in their complaints.

A similar stage has been theorised in relation to other 'pioneering' therapeutic communities. Reflecting on a TC in Amstelland, Holland, Van den Langenberg and de Natris (1985) called this the 'Magic Mountain' fantasy. The fantasy bolsters and exaggerates the self-esteem of a team struggling with outside pressures but can result in over-rating internal processes within the community at the expense of its relationship to the outside world (Hinshelwood 1987). This can result in obscure and esoteric formulations:

> It is as if they say: 'We up here are so exclusively involved in a unique process that we don't have to bother about all those futilities of daily life down there'. (Van den Langenberg and de Natris 1985, p.98)

This certainly seems to fit some of the descriptions of Paddington during the mid-1970s and specifically its emphasis on looking 'inwards' following the focus on an 'external enemy' during the campaign (Hall 1979):

> Many of the staff felt that most of the patients had undoubtedly benefited from the involvement excited by the protest, but both groups now considered it time to get back to the business of therapy, their prime objective. Although the majority of staff believed that participation in the fight had been therapeutic for the patients, they now began to argue that it was much easier to fight the external aggressor than to understand their intangible inner conflicts. (Baron 1984a, p.41)

In this 'enlightenment' stage, Hobson suggests that although there are grave dangers of community disintegration, there are also creative possibilities that could prevent the move to the third stage of disintegration. However, a failure to recognise that the original idealisation was a mistake can result in the third and last stage, 'the catastrophe'.

Here, the cultural adage 'what goes up, must come down' is recast psychodynamically as the process of idealisation to denigration. Thus Goodburn was both an initiator, and victim, of the process in this narrative. Massaged by his success in the campaign, Goodburn's status as the pinnacle of self-knowledge, charismatic leader and innovator, if left unchallenged, could only lead to disaster. In this final stage, the charisma of the leader wears thin and the special abilities that he and the community are imagined as possessing are seen as a sham. Again, Baron's narrative illustrated this process at Paddington where she argued that:

> because they had so richly endowed him (the Medical Director) with special power, his fall from grace, when it came, was felt particularly strongly by his earlier admirers. (1984a, p.90)

During this stage, expectations of the leader and the TC itself are recognised as having been illusory and the group fantasy is shattered. Hobson (1979) argued that this phase is often marked by group disturbances and 'acting out' such as violence, suicide and secret sexual relationships. It can result in the death of the community, its disintegration or collapse and serious damage to its members, including serious psychological breakdowns – especially in prominent members of staff. At this time other therapeutic communities could also be seen to be experiencing serious consequences of the failure of the messianic fantasy. At both Marlborough Day Hospital and Claybury the head consultants in charge of the hospitals committed suicide, perhaps the most pertinent indicator of Hobson's 'catastrophe' (Hinshelwood 1979). Similarly, Hinshelwood presented a paper at the Annual Association of Therapeutic Communities in 1979 using W.R. Bion's warning about the messiah who is not supposed to appear and the real life-and-death consequences if he does appear. However, as we shall explore further in the next chapter, although Paddington certainly experienced a significant breakdown, things did not happen in quite such an extreme way.

## Protest, radicalism and therapeutic communities

The accounts I have discussed above provide useful cautionary tales and draw attention to the tensions and dynamics between protest, social movements and the development of TCs. They caution against the problems and dangers of raising high expectations and the difficulties arising in the aftermath of political protest. Furthermore, elements that are essential in fostering protest and developing social movements – such as positive feelings of power, solidarity, optimism and idealism – can be problematic and 'one sided' in terms of sustaining a therapeutic community practice. However, although these are important considerations, just re-reading the Paddington events as an example of 'asylum to anarchy' or 'idealisation to catastrophe' is deeply problematic if we are to hold on to the important possibilities of innovation and social change that these events gave rise to.

For example, during the protest at Paddington, explorations of wider dynamics and empowerment were possible, and therapeutic work continued but developed a structure appropriate to fighting a campaign (Goodburn 1976, 1986). In one sense this was necessary: in order for the therapeutic work to continue the day hospital needed to survive, and so needed a campaign. During this time an awareness of some of the conflicts inherent in the approach at Paddington may have temporarily been pushed to one side. At the same time, other dynamics and processes flourished, such as consciousness-raising, collective empowerment and group identification. The story of the development of the MPU at Paddington attests to the fact that we need to be able to account for radicalisation and protest as both a positive and creative force, rather than just a negative product of idealism.

As well as suggesting that the protests created the conditions for the later crisis, Baron's account also draws our attention to the links between the protest and the subsequent ability of patients to complain. Thus, as Baron argued, the fact that some of the patients had already been involved in the earlier protest (and those who had not felt that they had 'inherited the political will of their predecessors') helped to enable them to act as a unified force (1987, p.240). Although it is unclear how much impact the MPU had on the formulation of the complaints and the demand for an inquiry, at least one MPU member, Eric Irwin, was still attending Paddington and was one of the complainants during its crisis. Given the success and memory of the protest, when the day hospital did not meet people's expectations, many patients experienced disappointment and anger and were just as likely to turn their dissatisfaction on the day hospital itself and demand something better:

> Having been so active in their support of the hospital's primary goal, they were equally active in their rebuttal of the approach once they had come to define it as counterproductive to their own aims and interest. Better able than others to express themselves in therapy, they also had greater facility in airing their grievances. (Baron 1987, p.156)

Furthermore, the notion that the campaign fed into a growing idealisation of Paddington misses the complexity of the debates that occurred during the protests (Benn 1972; Haddon 1979; Smith 1972). It is important to remember that there was a complex negotiation of strategies and debates in the campaign, and the more political or idealistic activists were actually wary of an emphasis on psychotherapy as the 'solution'. Difficulties around charismatic leadership and idealisation can be viewed as much as a result of an over-reliance on psychoanalysis generally in TCs as it was a result of politicisation.

The TC movement is renowned for its reliance on charismatic leaders, and the origins of individual TCs are often linked specifically with the individual psychoanalytically trained or inspired psychiatrist at the helm (Pines 1999). The 'charisma' of Maxwell Jones (one of the key 'founders' of TCs) was seen as enabling an 'experimental credit' that gave TCs a space in which to form and develop (Manning 1991). In addition, so-called charismatic leaders have also been a source of inspiration for radical psychiatry. However, the initiation and leadership of most TCs and radical anti-psychiatric initiatives by charismatic male psychiatrists has often plagued many of these initiatives with ongoing tensions and difficulties (Parker *et al.* 1995; Showalter 1987). See Clancy Sigal's (1976) *Zone of the Interior* for a powerful fictionalised example of this.

However, it is also necessary to recognise the potentially important function of the radical charismatic leader. Radical innovators and radical innovations could be said to occupy a 'paradoxical space' in which they simultaneously subvert and reproduce prevailing power relations. It is such a paradoxical position that R.D. Laing occupied, highlighted in the title of a recent edited publication *R.D. Laing: Creative Destroyer* (Mullan 1997). Indeed, the tensions between such leaders' role in provoking challenge and providing inspiration and yet providing security, support and sustainability is an ongoing issue (Hinshelwood 1980).

Charismatic leadership often forms the basis of the origination of initiatives that welcome change, uncertainty and risk (Alaszewski, Manthorpe and Walsh 1995). In particular, 'innovative counterleaders' (Melucci 1996) seem to pick up on, and embody, a number of contradictions and tensions in the social world. Such leaders personally occupy and command social spaces available for social innovation. However, in creating the conditions for social change and making challenges that rub against the grain, they create resistance and controversy. Burston (1996) uses the notion of a 'trickster', a Jungian archetypal figure in world mythology to describe innovators like R.D. Laing, who challenged social and psychiatric conventions through their practice, lifestyle and persona.

The trickster is a contradictory force, both constructive and destructive. On a positive level it can be an agent of change and renewal, forcing us to confront unpalatable truths, raising awkward questions and challenging our conceptions of normality and acceptability. On the flip side, this maverick figure can produce unpleasant and shocking effects, and is experienced as both constructive and destructive. A figure that embodies and acts out various social tensions, pushing the limits of what is both possible and desirable is bound to have a variety of mixed effects. Thus Leon Redler recalls meetings with R.D. Laing as 'fundamentally (and paradoxically) without supports, unpredictable, disturbing, heartening, inspiring, awe-ful and/or aweful' (in Burston 1996, p.2).

Through attempting to gain understanding of the crisis or breakdown at Paddington we can acquire a unique insight into some of the difficulties in forging radical and democratic TCs. It is important, therefore, to gain an accurate understanding of the complex dynamics between radical action and therapeutic practice. However, while the narratives of asylum to anarchy and idealisation to catastrophe are important and useful, they do not sufficiently articulate the radical impulse that drove Paddington and the attempts that were made to forge alternative practices and relationships. Most importantly, such accounts do not address the elements within TCs that were expressions of the broader developments that generated innovative mental health politics. Radical, innovative practices and charismatic figures can leave behind wider social spaces, potentially expanding political and therapeutic possibilities. Unfortunately, the space left behind after the demise of Paddington ultimately closed down the potential for innovation and change in TCs. However, this was not simply because of the particular difficulties at Paddington, but was also a consequence of how the events at Paddington have been constructed by observers and commentators subsequently.

# CHAPTER SEVEN

# A Consumable Pill of History

Although the wider authorities and some patients themselves found the nature of the practice at Paddington extremely challenging and unsettling, the dominant version of events has failed to take full account of some of the more progressive elements of Paddington. The previous chapter described two accounts of crisis and decline in a TC (Hobson's 'Messianic Community' and Baron's *Asylum to Anarchy*). In the case of Paddington I argue that these two narratives have become synthesised into one dominant narrative. This dominant account of the decline of Paddington has tended to minimise and problematise the role of political action and radical aspirations. This chapter explicitly challenges that dominant narrative and explores how it effectively pathologised Paddington and closed down possible alternative readings and accounts. It examines the construction of Paddington by its critics at the time, by the inquiry and by later commentators and tries to find a different way of interpreting these events in which important radical strands are not simply written out or pathologised.

## Asylum to anarchy as a culturally available narrative

Baron's *Asylum to Anarchy* is convincingly written, and well evidenced – so much so that the eventual outcome seems necessary and inevitable. However, in accepting this account as the 'real' account of Paddington, we are also invited to accept other possible truths that seem to naturally flow from the narrative. Using the work of critical historians such as Hayden White (1986, 1996, 1999), this section explores how the narrative arising from Baron's account was socially constructed as a contained narrative that functioned as a consumable pill of history, one that was both culturally available and satisfying. Although this narrative was uncomfortable to hear, its construction managed to present digestible conclusions that have been used to justify caution about radical innovation and experimentation in TCs.

Critical historians have argued that all historical accounts are shaped by the historian, who is embedded in a specific social and historical context (Jenkins 1991). Historical accounts are not only a construction of the past, but also a construction of the present – a device through which we launch our current enquiry and reach back to describe past events. Viewing the past through the cultural filters of the present is essential in the construction of a narrative that can resonate with, and be understood within, the reader's current cultural referents. White (1999) argues that history is structured as combinations of facts and events, which the historian frames within a fictional structure or narrative. He argues that we can only gain a coherent comprehension of events if they are organised in such a way as to display features that are recognisable from stories or genres that are culturally available.

When histories do resonate with contemporary cultural narratives they are easier to remember and circulate. It is this 'story-value' that gives historical accounts meaning and plausibility. It also gives accounts ideological value and 'fixes' the significance or 'reading' of events, thereby giving them an explanatory framework (Carroll 1998). However, White (1999) argues that there are actually only a limited number of generic story types available at any given time. This means that the reception of a given history depends as much – if not more – upon the widespread availability of these stories as on their accurate correspondence with the events themselves. For histories to 'work' they require unity, coherence 'emplotment' and fulfilment.

> Truth must be allied to a narrativisation, a plot which reconstitutes the historical and subjective dimension of lived experience, by locating events in a 'configuration' of events, as part of a story line which evokes the presence of the past in the present. (Venn 1992, p.58)

White's conception of the construction of history can help to explain the construction of the dominant narrative that was drawn on to account for the events at Paddington. For example, Claire Baron's account reflected a particular narrative that was persuasive in its appeal because of the cultural referents it contained. Baron's account is so influential that it would be wise to examine its construction more closely in order to understand its power to persuade a TC audience. We can see the influence of Baron's work in the comments of two key participants at Paddington:

> This psychotherapist who teaches occupational therapy students says, 'Ah yes, the Baron book, of course it's a classic text'. Classic text of what, do you know? Of where, of who, where's the dialogue about it? (Thomas 2000)

But you know, why are people so prepared to receive this as wisdom?...Claire
Baron would surely be preaching to the converted. You know, it could hardly
be received wisdom unless it struck a chord...it would have to be there, ready
and waiting, wouldn't it?...it obviously met a need... The fact that it isn't
challenged, isn't taken to bits, and that it was readily received and
greeted...a myth that's convenient to those receiving it, the vast majority.
(Goodburn 2000)

Baron's account drew upon a pervasive and popular narrative of 'tragedy' and
radical failure. *Asylum to Anarchy* is a compelling read; it provides a satisfying
denouement in that we receive a coherent and recognisable picture of decline
and ultimate defeat for a radical project. However, in telling the story of a TC
that went from 'asylum to anarchy' or 'idealisation to catastrophe', it offers us
a more linear narrative than may actually be warranted. The following section
questions some of the assumptions within this dominant narrative of radical
failure and decline.


## Disputing catastrophe

While the dominant narrative was of chaos and extreme bad practice, this
section questions whether the Paddington events did, in fact, constitute a 'catastrophe' (Hobson 1979), 'disaster' (Sandison 1982) or 'tyranny' (Baron
1987). Indeed, one could argue that in the light of catastrophes discussed
elsewhere (Hobson 1979; Hinshelwood 1979), Paddington does not emerge
as an excessively disastrous experiment.

Undoubtedly, there were difficult incidents at Paddington. However,
during my research it became apparent that there were disputed interpretations of these incidents and the actual level of risk was often exaggerated. For
example, although the official inquiry had been alerted to the possibility of
violence, an investigation into the dangers of violence in the day hospital concluded that 'there was no more danger of violence there, in fact probably less,
than in other comparable units elsewhere' (KCWAHA 1976, p.24). Crocket
observed that violence had been 'contained', which was 'an important
achievement at a clinical level' (1978, p.14). However, rising opposition to the
practices at Paddington and assumptions about the 'unsuitability' of the
patient group often resulted in misinformation and over-reaction. For
example, notes from a meeting at Paddington recorded an instance when the
Chairman of the Paddington Centre mistook a patient holding a screwdriver
(in order to fix something in the day hospital) for a knife and subsequently
wrote a letter to the area health authority about the potential danger in the

day hospital. Goodburn (1986) argued that although there *were* incidences of patients 'acting out' their frustrations during this period, there were also increasingly wild and inaccurate rumours circulating of drug taking, sexual orgies, drunkenness and violence.

There were reports of one suicide at Paddington. Baron (1984a) specifically refers to a woman patient who, after attending Paddington for a short while, left and some time later was heard to have committed suicide. However, the details of this were unclear – not least if, or how, her later suicide was related to her experience at Paddington. Apart from this incident, there were no reported suicides or serious suicide attempts of Paddington patients or staff. When one former staff member, who went on to be highly critical of radical developments within Paddington, was asked if there had actually been any suicides, he replied that 'rather surprisingly', there had been none (Anon 2000). Given the high suicide rate amongst people with a psychiatric diagnosis (Harris and Barraclough 1997) and those recently in touch with psychiatric services (Pirkis and Burgess 1998), this is not insignificant. Although there appear to have been two reported suicide *attempts* in the run up to the Paddington inquiry (Baron 1984a), without evidence from the patients these attempts can be interpreted in conflicting ways. If we accept the prevailing accounts of Paddington we would probably conclude that these attempts resulted from the damage inflicted by the day hospital regime upon patients. However, dissenters and supporters of Paddington saw these attempts and minor outbreaks of violence as a manifestation of patients' response to the way Paddington was treated by the authorities, and patients' fear of losing it. As one former worker recalled:

> One day [a patient] came to the clinic and he went to every window with his head. He broke the window like a bull, every window. And I had to drag him away... Another patient he was there only six months when things happened. He came in every week [to] kick the door or window, break it and then go. And then once they had to call the police. Next time he did it I confronted him and I saw him individually...and said 'you tell me what is happening?' ... He said 'The reason I'm breaking the window or the door is because that's what they did to the place I trusted, and I wanted to be in. They shattered all my life'. Obviously he was also projecting something, but still, that was the reaction about what happened to the place. (Jenner 2000)

Another contested issue was that of cleanliness. Most accounts of Paddington seem to agree that the day hospital was not being cleaned and was often very messy. Indeed, this was one of the complaints lodged by the patients and was obviously a real concern for patients and staff. However, reactions to this issue outside the day hospital raised more emotive and fearful concerns, such as the idea that the lack of cleanliness indicated that 'psychotic' or 'dangerous' forces were being unleashed at Paddington. This was most clearly articulated by the notion of patients 'smearing faeces' around the day hospital. In his unpublished autobiography, Rosen claimed that patient numbers dwindled and so, to keep numbers up, they included chronic schizophrenics, who smeared faeces on the walls but the consultant refused to allow the walls to be cleaned (1996). However, some interviewees suggested that this rumour had arisen when a small group of patients made clay faeces in the art room as a message to the community.

> There was also an art therapy department on the far end of the corridor of the same floor, which involved the same group of patients…it functioned in an autonomous fashion pretty much… And they had clay and a kiln there. And at one point somebody smeared clay – it didn't smell, you see, I mean I knew it wasn't shit – and wrote 'Cack' underneath it…on the wall opposite the toilet… I didn't really understand that that was an issue, that people really did think there was real shit smeared… I didn't really sort of make sense how significant it was until much later. (Goodburn 2000)

This cleaning issue was one of the pivotal issues in the life of Paddington. While it is undeniable that the day hospital was dirty and may have felt intolerable to some, the events were more complex than these accounts assumed. The dominant account at the time was that Paddington became so chaotic, filthy and unhygienic that something had to be done about it. However, first, the extent of the 'dirt' and other transgressions appear to have been exaggerated. Second, the cleaning issue actually arose in response to numerous complex factors that reflected structural constraints, issues of power and authority and even considerations of racial oppression and sexism.

As we have seen, Goodburn's decision not to replace the cleaner was partially an attempt at challenging patients' disrespect of the previous female black cleaner by ensuring that patients took responsibility for their own behaviour in the day hospital. While the way this decision was made was not as consultative as it perhaps should have been (as Goodburn himself admitted), the impulse behind it challenged orthodox psychiatric practice. It was part of a more wider ranging attempt to challenge the illness model by refusing to collude with patients' inherited status as passive patients. Indeed, this impulse to deal with the situation as a community was very much in accordance with TC theory and practice. Nevertheless, in retrospect it has been the supposed chaos and dirtiness of Paddington that is remembered rather than these radical impulses and ideas.

## Pathologisation

We have seen how idealisation may have become a problem in the day hospital following the successful protests that marked Paddington out as a radical alternative to traditional medicalised psychiatry. We saw how this has also been seen as a potential negative outcome of other campaigns to defend TCs from closure (Robinson 1994). Although this is an important consideration, it is also worth considering how one of the ways in which Paddington was pathologised was by viewing it merely as a product of idealism following heightened politicisation. It is possible that reactions to Paddington helped to undermine it through condemnations of its political ideologies and the subsequent pathologisation of staff and patients as well as the practice of the day hospital.

More generally, pathologisation has often been used in psychoanalysis as a strategy to marginalise political dissent (Leitner 1999). Leitner has illustrated how the attribution of psychopathology has been used extensively to discredit dissenters and has been a 'customary and a pervasive way of dealing with all kinds of problems in the psychoanalytic movement' (p.481). Moreover, the discrediting of alternatives in psychiatry has also resorted to political and personal patholgisation. For example, psychiatric opposition to the Italian democratic psychiatry movement denounced their activists and supporters as 'psychotic', and dismissed them as 'Marxists, Foucauldians, Fascists and Anarchists' (Kendall 1996).

At Paddington, specific concerns were raised about the political nature of the ideas and activities that were developing in the day hospital, such as the campaign against closure and the formation of the MPU. There was a concern that the day hospital was being used for overtly political and even revolutionary purposes. Moreover, in accounts of the Paddington crisis and decline the previous period of politicisation (the protests/MUP) was often drawn upon in assessing what 'went wrong'. The inquiry report referred to its previous struggle for existence as part of its 'chequered past' (KCWAHA 1976). Basil Gregory (Goodburn's predecessor at Paddington), stated in a letter to the chair of the Paddington Centre that he thought the first sign of the crisis was the political campaign and protest. Political recriminations about Paddington may have been related to the fact that the rest of the Centre was trying to market psychoanalysis to mainstream psychiatry and was concerned about its reputation and developing notoriety following the campaign.

A sense of the extent of the pathologisation of Paddington can be gleaned from the impression that Richard Crocket (1978) received when he arrived to take over as consultant after Goodburn was dismissed. He noted that the Paddington Centre as a whole seemed to be stratified (in fantasy) by many onlookers and participants according to its status and worth. He felt that this representation mapped onto the actual way in which the different departments in the centre were organised on different floors. That the day hospital occupied the lowest floor was convenient to the way it was represented and viewed by others as the lowest in status. He conceptualised this such that the top floor which housed the Child Guidance Clinic was seen as 'Heaven = Good'; the first floor (Adult Psychotherapy) as 'Middle Class/Mankind = Good' and the Ground Floor (Day Hospital) as 'Lower Class/Hell = Bad/Evil'.

Similarly, Goodburn (1976) commented that the day hospital was viewed as 'black', and like an 'unruly refugee from the East End' in the eyes of the rest of the Paddington Centre and the wider psychiatric establishment. This comment can be related to the idea that forms of racism produce notions of 'black' as being unruly, dangerous and dirty and that such associations often figure in public and media perceptions about mental health clients (Neal 1998; Spector 2001; Walker, Burman and Gowrisunkur 2002). Discussions around 'mental illness' and dangerousness may evoke notions of 'race' in public imagination without actually identifying race itself or even the presence of black people (Gillman 1985; Neal 1998).

These divisions weren't only symbolic representations but also related to very real material deprivations and structural divisions in the centre. In addition to the constant external threat (real and perceived) following the successful protest, Paddington was constantly uncertain as to its future, suffered a lack of space, and was reputedly insufficiently heated. In addition, dual appointments between the adult department and the day hospital often meant that staff had less time to spend in the day hospital. Furthermore, (as we saw in Chapter Five) Crocket (1978) thought that the lack of autonomy and independence of the day hospital was a key factor in its demise.

The unsuitability of the day hospital patients themselves was often also drawn upon in justifying the condemnation of Paddington. According to some observations, this was related to both the nature of the patients' mental health needs as well as their perceived social status and disposition. Some staff members felt that the apparent severity of patients' 'illness' or 'behavioural problems', and assumptions about their unsuitability for psychotherapy, may have contributed to the pathologisation of the day hospital. Goodburn (1976) recalled how patients were often seen as poor, working class and difficult, and viewed as 'noisy and uncouth'. Colleagues in the centre worried that individual patients attending for adult out-patient psychotherapy elsewhere in the centre would have to 'run the gauntlet of a disputatious, aggressive, or even destructively bizarrely dressed group on the way up' (Crocket 1978, p.19). As another staff member pointed out:

They were not your standard psychotherapy patients, you see. This is the crux of the matter I think. Those were not the people that they would want to see walking in and out of their sessions or small groups. Those people would have been selected out. (Thomas 2000)

In addition, patients supposed 'unsuitability' was often related to the lack of specific structures and procedures at Paddington – for example, the relaxation of its admission criteria; its reluctance to engage in detailed individual assessments and 'risk assessments'; and the preference for patients to negotiate their attendance between themselves; in effect, operating more like a 'drop-in'. Such developments did not fit well with traditional psychoanalytic or psychiatric ideas and practices.

In addition, the quest for greater democratisation was accompanied by the admirable attempt by staff to involve patients in as many aspects of the functioning of the day hospital as possible. Although the idea of 'user involvement' in the planning, provision and funding of services is now actively promoted in mental health services, at this time attempts to hand over greater responsibility, if not control, to patients was more unusual and even condemned. Thus the fact that staff had wanted patients to possess door keys to the day hospital was viewed as another example of the extreme nature of Paddington practice (Lemlij *et al.* 1979). Similarly, Goodburn's attempt to record the proceedings of the inquiry for the benefit of the patients was deemed inappropriate, excessive and used as confirmation of his wayward behaviour and practice.

During the official inquiry, Goodburn's own mental health state was questioned by the board, who reported that he was 'in a state of agitation' and decided to terminate their interview with him 'on medical grounds' (KCWAHA 1976, Appendix C). Indeed, Goodburn has often been singled out as the key pathological factor at Paddington. Following his dismissal Baron commented that 'although the patients at the day centre and those in the Area Health Authority were henceforth *protected from him*, others were not' (Baron 1984a, p.126, my emphasis).

Here it is possible to see the convergence of both political and psychological pathologisation. Back in 1971, during Goodburn's interview for the post of consultant/medical director, he was explicitly asked about his political views and affiliations and whether he would give the names of any Marxist political activists present in the day hospital. Goodburn had been influenced and inspired by some of the new ideas that were being discussed in the day hospital, particularly during the protests, and this already raised suspicion as to his suitability for the post. Although Goodburn objected to these questions and, with the aid of the General Medical Council, returned for a second interview and was eventually appointed (albeit on a more part-time basis than was the case in the post as originally advertised), his reputation as a radical didn't always endear him to others in the centre. This served to reinforce a developing division between the 'radicals' and 'conservatives'. Meanwhile Goodburn, who flourished on challenge and controversy, was determined to pursue the development of his ideas in the day hospital with or without the support of the rest of the centre.

However, one worker recalled how the combination of political and individualised pathologisation resulted in her more positive views of Paddington being continually silenced:

> After the day hospital had gone, some analysts wanted to dissociate themselves from it...if you tried to say something good about the day hospital... I learned that immediately people would attack you...and try to marginalise you. They thought you are the 'enemy of the state' if you like... We had an Open Day...in 1981...and I met one of the consultants... He had been on the [Inquiry] when Julian was going to answer to the Panel, and he said to me 'Oh yes, it was a terrible place the day hospital. It never functioned. And Julian was a communist and we had to get rid of him.' That's what he said! (Jenner 2000)

There were obviously many factors that contributed to the ease with which a negative narrative about the day hospital became possible. Their patients seemed different to those who usually engaged in psychotherapy and often had more complex or challenging needs. The political nature of the protest and the beliefs of some staff members and patients meant that challenges could be dismissed as part of a pre-existing political agenda and Goodburn himself scapegoated. However, despite this condemnation, there were some participants who saw the possibilities that had been opened up by Paddington's practice.

## Marginalisation of positive accounts

Positive accounts of Paddington were marginalised and lost in the construction of the dominant narrative of disaster and tyranny. Hinshelwood (1977) reported that the inquiry into Paddington was 'too one-sided' and he was concerned to balance it with some positive aspects. Equally, some of the workers who had been at Paddington during this period still highly valued their experience. For them, it was often the very factors that were condemned by onlookers that they found to be most beneficial and valuable. The following staff member argued that the lack of formal structures and the libertarianism were actually empowering in enabling staff and patients to develop additional activities:

> We would work well at that time. First, I think it was that minimum structure. Secondly we had this director who was supportive of what we did, and he was always supportive and protective if we had any problems…he gave a lot of freedom to the staff. I know it was supportive…Julian would say nothing. He said 'if you want to do your own thing you can', I think that was very important. (Jenner 2000)

For these staff members it was precisely the fact that the day hospital was able to work with such a diverse group of patients, who would usually have been deemed unsuitable for psychotherapy, that was so inspiring. They mounted a specific counter-discourse in defence of Paddington, drawing on its ability to work with difficult and disturbed clients:

> I was very sceptical when I came to this situation about analysis, psychoanalysis, anything that was going on, you know group analysis, all that. But I learned. I was open, my mind was open to learn. And I felt it was a great thing…I thought it was a great thing for these people [who] there was no hope for them, because they managed to actually live outside, at night going home, week-ending at home, looking after themselves, taking minimal drugs, medication…and at the same time living and talking about their feelings, just by talking. And we just needed a chair and a space and people… We didn't need anything else really. And it worked. And I was amazed, being so young…I was amazed the way these people's lives – and even people with personality disorders – they came in, they flourished. (Jenner 2000)

Indeed, Crocket noted that Paddington had established a permissive group culture for a number of patients with 'long-term personality problems' who had been able to achieve important relationships within the day hospital that would not have been possible within more conventional psychiatric institutions (1978, p.8). In particular, the libertarian approach at Paddington enabled the expression, and acceptance, of creativity, spontaneity, and eccentricity in the patient group. This expression, which would have been disapproved of in other settings, was nurtured and valued in the atmosphere of the day hospital and it became a place where some expressions of individuality and creativity could flourish:

The level of eccentricity...I think is another thing that's missing from any kind of record. There were some wonderful people. I mean there was a guy who changed his costume by the day, and it was another sort of form of performance. He had, like – I don't know if you remember those pyjama cases you used to get in the shape of furry toys. They had a zip down the back, you kept your pyjamas in them. He used to carry one of those as a handbag, and have sort of woolly brooches of a little dog with two puppies on a chain. It was sort of high kitsch stuff, and very flamboyant... Somebody came in and played saxophone solos. Others, you know, seemed to be able to recite free-form poetry, tell the stories about their lives. Nobody stopped them, it was terrific... There was a woman as well, a Jamaican woman...who used to wear totally transparent dresses, and would [stand at the] bus queue on the Harrow Road. And they'd be absolutely stunned. So you got people who really caught the eye in no uncertain way. (Thomas 2000)

In accepting and not pathologising these individual differences, the day hospital challenged conventional psychiatric and psychotherapeutic practices and demonstrated an awareness that in many ways was ahead of its time. Such thinking would not be out of place in contemporary thinking about the acceptance and celebration of diversity. The idea of celebrating expressions of 'mad culture' has recently been promoted by users and survivors of psychiatry and exemplified by organisations such as 'Mad Pride' in the UK (Curtis *et al.* 2000). In addition, while the numbers of women at Paddington dwindled, marginalised sexualities such as male homosexuality were expressed more readily (Crocket 1978), suggesting that these were becoming more acceptable. It is notable that homosexuality was frequently pathologised in psychiatric services during this time (Bayer 1987).

Despite these more positive aspects, the dominant narrative of Paddington as well as its condemnation and marginalisation, helped to reproduce certain notions of what is acceptable in therapeutic communities and psychiatric services in general. More specifically, some of the reactions to Paddington reinforced precisely those cultural perceptions of people designated 'mentally ill' that Paddington tried to challenge.

## Reinforcing notions of psychiatric acceptability

Concerns raised about Paddington in general came from a variety of sources and were not necessarily predicated on shared assumptions or values. However, concerns tended to rely upon certain psychiatric expectations and standards such as psychiatric assessments, note-taking, follow up and adequate referral procedures, and these figured strongly in the official enquiries. What forms a fundamental and recurring theme in the inquiry report into Paddington practice are continual references to what is 'acceptable' within the NHS 'for the practice of medicine'. The report deemed it unacceptable not to register patients, not to take clinical notes including patient history, diagnosis and treatment plan. It insisted that medical or nursing staff be on duty at all times (KCWAHA 1976) and stated that there were insufficient details on patients' risk, assessments and psychiatric reports. In addition, standards of cleaning were judged as insufficient for patients 'needing medical support' (p.20). The report concluded that the result was a situation that was not acceptable in a NHS hospital. This reinforced an overall medicalised framework of passive patients in need of medical assistance, which was precisely what the ideology of Paddington sought to challenge.

Doctors who were interviewed during the inquiry about the day hospital were 'unanimous in condemning what was going on in the day hospital' (KCWAHA 1976, p.27). Many staff within the Paddington Centre as a whole were increasingly concerned that the day hospital was breaking many accepted rules in both psychiatry and psychoanalysis and was having a disruptive effect on the centre as a whole. Minutes from official meetings at the time referred to their worries that the 'good names' of both psychoanalysis and psychiatry were being called into question by the work at Paddington and this was reiterated in the inquiry report. It is, of course, worth considering whether the contemporary practice of psychiatry at that time actually warranted their supposed 'good names'. Indeed, many of their practices and treatments have been seen as acceptable and appropriate at various times in the history of mental health intervention only later to be viewed with justified criticism (Breggin 1979, 1994; Johnstone 2000; Leifer 1969).

Furthermore, Goodburn was criticised by the inquiry for 'failing to carry out the duty of any consultant in the NHS' and his behaviour was considered remiss for having insufficient control 'over' patients under his care. (KCWAHA 1976, p.20) This criticism articulated a deep confusion both within Paddington and in responses to it. On the one hand, Goodburn was chastised for maintaining 'rigid autocratic control' (p.25) over patients through manipulation, and yet on the other hand he was criticised for *not* assuming enough control over patients' behaviour.

More generally, condemnation of Paddington invites scrutiny of how sanctions are imposed when defined limits are overstepped. Boundaries of acceptable practice often only become identified via transgressions or innovations. Accepted psychiatric practices operate as the central, reasonable subject against which otherness or unreason is defined and in turn, defines itself. If places of 'otherness' can function as the site of fantasy and myth, then they symbolise the possibility and threat of transgression (Venn 1992). Paddington crossed the boundaries of what was deemed proper and acceptable at that time. As Crocket pointed out, the official enquiries represented 'society at large' (1978, p.36). Such inquiries work to prescribe what elements are appropriate and desirable in particular settings. They therefore play a regulatory function by re-enforcing certain accepted knowledges and contributing to an understanding of the limits of transgression:

> If you don't play it by whatever rules, or by whatever codes of practice are seen as the usual way of doing things, or the established way of doing things…you're vulnerable… But, you know, fair enough. Because what's going to happen is that as the inquiry extends, it is going to be an inquiry into how authority functions. (Goodburn 2000)

## Dirt and purification

Since Paddington practice did contain some progressive elements, how did it come to be seen as so pathological? This section demonstrates how ideas of pollution, dirt and cleanliness were mobilised by a dominant psychiatric and therapeutic orthodoxy to discredit Paddington. It describes how responses and official reactions to the crisis at Paddington served to establish the 'danger' of the day hospital and a fear of the spread of some of the practices of Paddington – its potential for infection or contamination. One staff member recalled:

> I had left the Day Hospital, I had withdrawn to the adult out-patients department as the complaint had began to gather momentum, so I actually wasn't in there, [but] I could still smell it. (Anon 2000)

The 'smell' of Paddington Day Hospital referred to above is about more than actual dirt or cleanliness. It also symbolises wider socially sanctioned ideas about culturally appropriate behaviours and how these feed into the possibilities and limitations of experimentation and innovation in psychiatry. The social anthropologist Mary Douglas argues that beliefs about pollution, dirt and cleanliness are often mobilised in order to justify claims of status and worth (Douglas 1978). In the context of Paddington these ideas were mobilised to delineate the boundaries of the acceptable and so push Paddington beyond the bounds of 'normal' behaviour as defined by the dominant psychiatric establishment. Socially sanctioned inquiries and other official reactions can result in a process that separates, purifies, demarcates and punishes transgressions.

Looked at in this way, the official inquiries into Paddington exemplified 'rituals of purification' that clearly demonstrated the 'normal' and 'usual' ordering pattern of social systems and so provided a public and visible mechanism to ensure the maintenance of the social and psychiatric order. The inquiries can be seen as functioning as a purification process that served to highlight difference and emphasise marginality. Such 'social ordering' processes have as their main function the imposing of order onto an inherently untidy experience (Douglas and Wildavsky 1983) and as a result can create a greater apparent sense of order and agreement than is often in fact the case.

The acceptable reaction to Paddington became that of revulsion and condemnation. The day hospital was seen to require purification and cleansing, as well as separation and distance, in order to restore order and faith not only in TCs, but also in psychiatry and psychoanalysis in general. This purification process demanded the 'distancing' of Paddington from all good-thinking folk and, finally, the re-establishment of acceptable practice. As a result there followed a collective need to dissociate from Paddington following its crisis in order not to be tarnished by its reputation. A number of highly regarded analysts and clinicians renounced any support they had given Paddington and reported their sense of shame at being associated with it. Other staff in the centre expressed the view that it was making their discipline appear foolish by 'flying in the face of what is commonly understood about reality' (Baron 1984a, p.61).

It is important to recognise that the condemnation of Paddington was a social and historical judgement rather than an 'objective' ahistorical one. Evaluations and judgements of risk and acceptability are political, aesthetic and moral matters (Douglas 1992; Furedi 1997). The notion of what is 'commonly understood about reality' is contested not only by researchers, ethnographers and critical theorists, but by psychoanalysis itself, which suspends notions of external realities, and 'common sense' in its quest for hidden unconscious inner truths. Paradoxically, it is precisely by using notions of 'external reality' or 'common sense' that patients frequently resist and contest TC (and psychoanalytic) practices.

## Cautioning against innovation and experimentation

Related to the dominant story of disaster and eventual overthrow of tyranny, is a story about the dangers of failed radical experimentation. If dominant narratives function as one of the ways in which the past circulates and participates in the regulation of the present (Venn 1992), dominant accounts of

Paddington functioned to warn against the 'dangers' of innovation and experimentation and reinforce stories of radical failure. One function of Baron's *Asylum to Anarchy* was its cautioning against innovation and democratisation in mental health services. Indeed, Baron argues that her analysis 'seemed to illustrate the...irrationality of more democratic psychiatric methods' (1984b, p.157).

Moreover, in pathologising Paddington as 'anarchic', the theory and practice of anarchy itself is left undefined and unexplored, with it simply being equated with chaos, which is viewed as being an inevitably bad thing. It is worth examining this assumed negative value of 'anarchy' particularly as some have recently recommended exploring the positive connections between anarchy and TCs (Bowen and Staebler 2002; Glennister 2002). Unfortunately, like Baron, those making such recommendations do not fully define or explore the concept of anarchy. However, it is used positively in one instance to describe how a TC actually survived a crisis (Bowen and Staebler 2002). This is illustrated by the title of their short paper, 'A Living Testament to the Power of Anarchy', in a reversal of Baron's discourse. David Wills, one of the major British pioneers in therapeutic community work with children and young people thought that the term 'anarchy', far from meaning chaos or destructiveness, often describes the processes that occur within TCs, perhaps better so than vague notions of 'democracy' (Weaver 1962). However, Baron's use of 'anarchy' in an unquestioned way stirred up narratives of 'extremism', particularly of the left, that lead to barbarism and chaos. This drew upon, and fed into, available circulating stories of radical failure.

> It's almost like a kind of microcosmic version of the fall of 'socialism' in inverted commas, you know. 'It can't work, we've seen it, you know. They tried it in Russia, they tried it in Paddington and it's, you know, it's no good.' (Goodburn 2000)

The context within which the Paddington narrative gained credence was a wider political and cultural climate marked by a receding counter culture and the decline and demoralisation of the Left. The attacks on Paddington coincided with the rise of Thatcherism in the UK and subsequent attacks on trade unions and social movements. The defeat of the miners' strike in 1984/5 and the collapse of any remaining illusion in a 'socialist' Eastern Europe led many to become pessimistic about the possibility of the success of radical initiatives and social change more widely.

If innovation was dangerous then Paddington seemed to provide the 'evidence' of the need to bring in more conformity and regulation. Narratives of radical failure helped to justify the need to usher in greater conservatism in therapeutic communities and psychiatric services generally and this coincided with the rise of risk-aversive practices. The unacceptable risks that Paddington was seen to have taken converged with a growing sense of risk aversion, which has increased in recent years in psychiatry, TCs and society more generally (Castel 1991; Furedi 1997; Szmukler 2001). More significantly, because such reactions perform a standardising and centralising role (Douglas 1992), the fate of Paddington contributed to the greater standardisation of TC practices.

The effect of this cautionary tale was to narrow the space for alternative experimental initiatives. The narrative of *Asylum to Anarchy* permeated the consciousness of TC practitioners, and their tacit acceptance of certain of its assumptions went on to influence the direction of TCs. Hinshelwood reflected that:

> For many TC workers, and those who took the ATC forward, the Paddington became a signifier of the radical end of TCs and thus evidence of the need to move towards more a conformist political stance...[Paddington's] demise was a major prompt to TCs to draw back and re-examine permissiveness during the 1980s when the gains of the 1960s were being rolled back anyway by the Government...I think what others learned mostly was to go in the other direction, 180 degrees about turn... Yes it did make people think that innovation was dangerous and that we should bring in conformity into TCs. (Hinshelwood 2000)

In one sense, it matters little whether dominant accounts of Paddington were 'true' or not. What matters is the way they *functioned* in the history of psychiatric alternatives. In a debate in the *International Journal of Therapeutic Communities* Baron (1985) in fact argued that she was committed to radical innovation in NHS mental health services and did not condemn what was attempted at the day hospital.

In some ways, Baron's analysis is reminiscent of Jo Freeman's classic and highly influential pamphlet, 'The Tyranny of Structurelessness' (Freeman 1974). Freeman criticised the manipulative tendencies of unstructured political and feminist organisations of the time. She argued that organisational structurelessness can become a way of masking the power of the most powerful, whether they are conscious of their power or not. Thus the myth of structurelessness makes it hard to put limits on the use of power and it can become capricious. However, unlike Freeman, Baron's analysis lacked any broader political awareness and commitment. While Freeman's analysis arose out of, and contributed to, the development of the women's movement, Baron's *Asylum to Anarchy* was taken up by more reactionary forces. This was perhaps because her analysis wasn't embedded within, or linked to, a progressive social movement or analytical framework, although it is hard to disagree with Baron when she maintains:

> The sad thing was that [Paddington] failed and this failure played into the hands of those conservative elements in the National Health Service that feel that taxpayers' money should not be risked on more radical departures in the treatment of the mentally ill. (1985, p.118)

Just as sad perhaps was that Baron's account itself, and its reception, did little to redress this tendency. As mentioned earlier, events can be constructed into a narrative but the way in which this is done is constrained by the number of generic story types available at a given time and by the cultural and political climate of the time. Although each 'emplotment' applied to a given set of events opens up the opportunity for competing plot narratives (White 1996, 1999), the sequence of events at issue in Baron's book do not easily lend themselves to an alternative narrative. The absence of any readily available cultural narratives also make it hard to construct a more satisfying account. It is difficult to escape these narrativising cultural structures. Furthermore, the resources of emplotment and other standards of historical evaluation such as unity, comprehensiveness and coherence are not readily available in more complex non-linear accounts. Accounts that are not allied to a particular cultural narrative, or a sufficient counter discourse, are less satisfying, difficult to remember and less likely to mobilise remedial action. As a result they often only serve to inadvertently reinforce the legitimacy of available dominant stories. If *Asylum to Anarchy* was a 'culturally available narrative' we are left with the dilemma of what possibilities this affords for developing more progressive alternative narratives.

One alternative narrative might be that of a reversed tragedy. This would read as a plucky little day hospital battling for survival against the powers of the prevailing establishment and ideological forces. In this story, eventually the status quo reasserted itself and the agent provocateurs were expelled. However, although my narrative touches upon such a story at times, and, despite being a more satisfying narrative, it was not sufficient to make sense of the various complex events and accounts surrounding Paddington. I have tried not to reproduce stories about Paddington as either being just a disastrous experiment that had to be stopped or as an important innovation that was prevented from continuing. It may be that both of these sides contain some truth but a dialectical approach allows us to lay claim to both possibilities, rather than attempting to integrate or merge these conflicts and construct a more comfortable 'truth'.

In summary I would argue that the narrative of *Asylum to Anarchy* is insufficient to address development in TCs as expressions of broader developments in generating innovative mental health politics. Not only does it imply that innovation, radicalism and activism tend to reinforce dynamics of idealisation and catastrophe, it is also a uni-dimensional and ahistorical account. As a narrative it suited the particular political climate of the 1980s with its emerging emphasis in individual consumerism rather than collective organisation. Indeed, the moment when Goodburn was asked to 'choose' whether or not to replace the cleaner marked this important turn in the history of health and welfare services. The inquiry into the functioning of Paddington could even be viewed as a prototypical case of the opportunities and limitations resulting from contemporary consumerist ideology (Hinshelwood 2002). Paddington cannot be considered a model of 'good practice' and the importance of listening and responding to patients' complaints may have over-ridden any potential possibilities in the approach itself. Yet its closure and subsequent pathologisation closed off the pursuit of more progressive collectivised alternatives and reinforced dominant and medicalised conceptualisations of psychiatry.

Paddington was pathologised even though there was little evidence of any serious or catastrophic events during its existence. Despite this, the lessons that have been drawn from Paddington (like Kingsley Hall before it) was that too much libertarianism, structurelessness and permissiveness in TCs should be avoided and greater controls and regulations instituted. The next chapter considers some of the consequences of the implementation of these increased controls and regulations in TCs. I also argue that, far from being an aberration, Paddington actually provides a particular, and perhaps not that unusual, example of ongoing tensions in contemporary TCs.

# CHAPTER EIGHT

# Anarchy to Asylum?
# Ongoing Conflicts in Practice

The previous chapter described how Paddington was pathologised within dominant accounts as an extreme and unjustifiable departure from acceptable practice within psychiatry, psychotherapy and TCs. Although the narrative of asylum to anarchy functioned effectively to close down further discussion of the Paddington story, I would argue that the problems the day hospital experienced were not necessarily or primarily a result of its departure from accepted practices.

The crisis at Paddington resulted from a broad range of factors, not least the declining impetus of counter-cultural forces and progressive social movements during the 1970s. Another important contributory factor in the downfall of Paddington was the use of psychoanalysis as the dominant framework of understanding dynamics within the community itself. These psychoanalytic frameworks reframed radical questions and challenges from patients in increasingly individualised therapeutic terms, thereby negating their meaning and ultimately suffocating the possible development of more progressive ideas. This process of suffocation highlights a number of tensions within TC practices between collective decision-making and the use of psychoanalysis.

Both radical and more conventional TCs must find ways of managing these conflicts and it is arguable whether any particular approach has proved necessarily more successful than another. Moreover, the consequences of their diverse attempts at resolution still suffuse and frame contemporary TC practices. It has been argued that a useful task of researchers is to 'unpack and influence contemporary resolutions of paradox' (Rappaport 1986, p.141). The ways in which the broader paradoxes inherent in TC practice – between democracy and psychoanalysis – are resolved highlight ongoing dilemmas in the theory and practice of TCs. Although the difficulties at Paddington highlighted these dilemmas in a number of unique ways, as these difficulties are in themselves far from unique they do in fact illuminate the consequences of the problems more clearly.

## Democracy and psychoanalysis

Democracy and psychoanalysis are widely regarded by key TC theorists as the two founding principles of TCs and this certainly remains the case in adult mental health services the UK. As a result, TCs in this tradition (which has been termed the 'democratic therapeutic community') have had to find ways of dealing with the tensions between the twin and often opposing values and practices of psychoanalysis and democracy. Psychoanalysis has been described as the 'founding idea' of TCs and as such is central to the TC movement, which remains fundamentally attached to these psychoanalytic roots (Hinshelwood 1999). Equally, TCs are often defined in relation to their similarity to, or extension of, group analysis. In turn, group analysis is heavily influenced by psychoanalysis and seen in many quarters as an important part of the broader spectrum of psychoanalytic practice today (Dalal 1998; Rawlinson 1999). While many TCs no longer use psychoanalysis quite as explicitly as Paddington did, psychoanalytic thinking still permeates contemporary TC practices – by which I mean the continued use of psychodynamic ideas and concepts derived from psychoanalysis. Although TCs are often 'blended' with other psychological influences including humanistic (e.g. Byrt 1999) and cognitive behavioural therapies (e.g. Rawlinson 1999), psychoanalytic thinking still remains the predominant framework used to understand interpersonal dynamics in TC. While Kennard claims that psychoanalytic training is 'almost entirely irrelevant for TC work and Group Analytic training is only partially relevant', he recognises that this observation is rarely acknowledged in practice (Kennard 1998, p.146).

Psychoanalysis wields considerable power within Western society, both as a therapeutic technique and a wider cultural resource that is embedded in structures, discourses and hierarchies of power (Parker 1997; Proctor 2002). The power, prestige and nature of psychoanalytic expertise can result in it being hard to challenge, in part because of its reliance on notions of the unconscious. In addition, the linguistic dominance of psychoanalytic conceptualisations within TCs can result in a continuation of unchallenged power structures, whether or not the boundaries or limits of staff decision-making powers are made clear to patients. Although multiple, interwoven and conflicting discourses inevitably exist in therapeutic institutions such as TCs, psychoanalytical knowledge usually prevails, by virtue of those possessing psychoanalytic expertise having linguistic as well as institutional power (Wodak 1996).

In this context, despite the twin influences of democracy and psychoanalysis, it is not perhaps surprising that psychoanalysis frequently becomes the privileged framework. Psychoanalytic ideas can be helpful in many contexts, including TCs – as the earlier history of Paddington demonstrates. However, this usefulness arose from psychoanalysis being developed in the context of a wider social and political project in which psychoanalysis influenced, but did not determine, practice. The tendency for psychoanalysis to operate as the most important and 'deeper' framework, particularly within contexts of lessened social awareness, is problematic. Although there is some acknowledgment within TC literature of the tensions and conflicts in linking therapeutic practice with democratic process, these tensions (and their consequences) remain insufficiently addressed or theorised.

This failure to examine these tensions contributes to the ease with which a more experimental TC like Paddington can be pathologised. Although Paddington was seen as a 'radical failure', in lots of ways it functioned no less effectively than many other more respectable or mainstream TCs that were also plagued with similar difficulties in managing the tension between democratic involvement and psychoanalytically informed practice. It was merely that the innovative nature of Paddington lent itself to scapegoating from more orthodox practitioners, who might have found it more uncomfortable to examine the basis of their own practice.

In order to demonstrate the ongoing tension between democratisation and psychoanalytic thinking in TCs it is necessary to examine more examples of contemporary TC practice. This chapter will therefore include some reflections on a piece of research I carried out in a modern, well-established contemporary non-residential TC in England (Spandler 2002). I will refer to this as the 'modern unit'. This research illustrates how the dilemmas and conflicts arising in this case study, and the ways in which they were managed, illustrated more general and ongoing difficulties across TCs. Moreover, as at Paddington, the modern unit's staff were explicitly trying to move towards greater levels of democratisation, and my research was partly informed by a shared commitment to understanding the possibilities and limitations of increased democratising practices. The research took the form of participant observation, a method of investigation often used in TC research (Bloor 1981; Bloor et al. 1988; Bloor and McIntosh 1990; Manning 1989; Rapoport 1960; Rawlings 1980; Sharp 1975; Sugerman 1975). Ethnographic, qualitative social research utilising participant observation that does not prioritise clinical concerns or 'outcomes' is seen as more in keeping with the philosophy and practice of the TC (Lees 1999). This method was also used by Baron in her research at Paddington, which facilitates a tentative comparison.

Baron (1984b, 1987) argued that it was the particular combination of, and over-emphasis on, psychoanalysis and democracy that led to (what she considered to be) anarchy, chaos and tyranny. The following sections specifically address the key elements of psychoanalysis and democracy at Paddington that Baron identified and then explore the ways in which similar tensions still suffuse modern TC practices.

## Rules and regulations

Baron (1987) described the particular way in which she thought Paddington implemented the notion of democratisation by basically abandoning rules and structures, and this became one of her major criticisms. She argued that without clear rules and regulations, staff were forced to rely on psychoanalytic interpretations as the main form of social control and regulation in the day hospital. The reliance on implied rather than overt rules made resistance and criticism extremely difficult. In particular, the apparently democratic mechanism of being able to bring any issues to the unstructured large group effectively resulted in the suppression of deviant opinion (1984a). The fact that the main 'currency' in the day hospital was psychoanalysis resulted in patients' criticisms being viewed simply as being pathologically motivated by their unconscious and as a result were either ignored or pathologised (1987).

In Baron's view (1984b, 1987), clearer rules and more formal structures are essential to facilitate more open disagreement and criticism. She claimed that if staff had been left with more formal authority they might not have resorted to more informal, psychoanalytic authority. At Paddington, Baron claimed there was a discrepancy between the ideology of democratisation and its reality, which essentially was not made explicit because a psychoanalytic hierarchy operated at a covert level to prevent challenge and criticism.

Yet if we look to the modern context we find that even when TCs have instituted tighter and more boundaried structures and regulations this doesn't necessarily prevent other difficulties. However, the difference lies in the way these difficulties are expressed and managed. In terms of the tension between patients' freedom and effective social organisation (Kennard 1982), Paddington arguably prioritised freedom at the expense of effective social organisation; it could be argued that modern-day TCs have the reverse problem. Although Baron's recommendation that TC staff need more formal power and

procedures has been incorporated into many TC practices, this has not necessarily solved the problems she raised.

In the modern unit, staff were developing strategies to define the boundaries of patients' involvement, and the formal authority of the staff team was
made more explicit. There was a more structured therapeutic programme and
clearer boundaries, as well as explicit rules and regulations. Although the
whole community had input into admissions and discharges, ultimately
gatekeeping into the community and final decisions regarding patients' use of
the unit was provided by the medical and therapeutic staff – and this included
detailed assessments and tight referral criteria. While Paddington attempted
to work with a variety of clients with mental health needs (including those
deemed unsuitable for traditional psychotherapy such as people with a
diagnosis of psychosis or schizophrenia), in the modern unit, a strict system of
referrals and assessments usually resulted in these potential patients not being
admitted.

In addition, clear guidelines and rules were also made available to new
patients to facilitate their therapy. For example, patients were requested not to
meet other patients outside the agreed community programme, and boundaries were strict and monitored by staff (and other patients). Behaviour considered as 'acting out', such as self-harm, unprescribed drug use, boundary
transgressions and lateness, were carefully monitored by staff. Patients were
encouraged to monitor their own, and others' behaviour and to report any
issues or transgressions. Boundary violations were regulated through formal
procedures such as suspensions, discharges and individuals being placed on
the community agenda to be discussed by the community. Patients were
required to attend all aspects of the unit's programme regularly and promptly
and to participate in ways that were considered therapeutic for themselves and
others. They were required to develop personal aims and objectives and take
part in regular reviews of their progress.

Paddington and the modern unit each suffered specific difficulties
relating to their particularly different, even opposing, ways of resolving the
same paradox between democracy and psychoanalysis. The crucial difference
between the two institutions lies in the consequences of the particular ways in
which these paradoxes were resolved. At Paddington, one of the benefits of a
more unstructured, unregulated and permissive culture was the creation of opportunities for greater creativity and spontaneity. In particular, this led to
spin-offs such as the patients' commune, the MPU and other activities that
were supported by Paddington staff. However, some patients found the more
libertarian and unstructured approach resulted in difficulties, with a lack of
care and support associated perhaps with a more 'adolescent' and rebellious

culture. For example, some patients at Paddington had complained that there was a lack of human response by the staff team. Another observer commented that ultimately it was the lack of 'caring for' people that became critical at Paddington (Kreeger 1981, p.232). As we have seen, this environment may have contributed to the dwindling attendance of women patients.

The more structured approach used in the modern unit may have differed from the earlier approach at Paddington, but it also had mixed consequences. On the one hand, while the lack of structure might have prevented women's participation at Paddington, the modern unit's more structured approach enabled staff to make decisions which could actually facilitate women's attendance. On the other hand, increasing regulatory practices, strict criteria, assessments, expulsions and clearer institution of boundaries in the modern unit resulted in a more paternalistic (or maternalistic) approach. The staff team in the modern unit were aware of unequal power relations within the patient group itself, for example the manner in which some men's behaviour may prevent the participation of women. This awareness provided a challenge to their ability to put into practice greater shared decision-making as they were reluctant to trust decisions arrived at collectively in case they were heavily influenced by particularly vociferous patients' views. Subsequently, it was partly the staff team's awareness of these dynamics that precipitated a series of seemingly 'undemocratic' decisions.

At Paddington, when Goodburn decided not to replace the cleaner as a misplaced but well intentioned gesture to challenge the patients' mistreatment of her, it exposed some of the problems inherent in the day hospital approach. Similarly, in the modern unit some of the staff team's decisions were well meant but also highlighted other difficulties in their approach and, in turn, led to other less desirable consequences. This doesn't mean in either case that their awareness of the problem was wrong or inaccurate, but that the theoretical resources they used to deal with it were inadequate.

For example, during a period of conflict in the modern unit, staff gave an 'ultimatum' to patients insisting that they either agree to work within their model, including the boundaries set by the staff and the rules and structures available to them, or leave. In effect, if they couldn't or wouldn't do this they would be discharged. Furthermore, staff made decisions as to who they considered able (or unable) to 'work therapeutically', in order to ensure that those attending the unit were committed and invested in the therapeutic programme and model. This was a clear assertion of their clinical authority by stating the importance of the therapists' interpretation of what was necessary therapeutically. The staff also made a decision to discharge a particularly 'difficult' patient even though this went against the will of the rest of the patient group.

Staff members felt that if they hadn't made these decisions it might have resulted in less participation and therapeutic benefit for other patients. In this
situation, some patients experienced a lack of freedom and felt infantilised
and constrained. Indeed, many patients argued that the unit's guidelines
themselves were often problematic and difficult to challenge – particularly the
structures of regulation, control and surveillance, which they regarded as
oppressive or punitive.

The most important 'evidence' of the difficulties and problems at Paddington was the fact that a number of patients complained about the way they
were being treated. Yet Paddington was far from being exceptional in having a
number of patients' complaining as complaints often figure in TC practices.
For example, during only a very short period of research at the modern unit,
approximately half of the patients signed a letter of complaint about the strict
regulations imposed on a number of patients in the community and lack of
patients' involvement in decision-making. In fact, this was the same propor-
tion of patients who complained at Paddington. Moreover, although it is hard
to make a direct comparison, while Paddington staff positively endorsed the
development of the MPU, at the modern unit an independent patients' group
set up by a number of the patients who had left, or were discharged, was not
well received by the staff.

These observations lead me to the conclusion that Paddington and the
modern unit used two different ways of resolving ongoing tensions between
democratisation and the use of psychoanalysis in TCs. At Paddington the
crisis continued until external regulatory forces intervened. Although
measures were taken to 'interpret' and understand the situation, no internal
structures or regulations were utilised, until the official inquiry. At the modern
unit, internal regulatory and procedural structures were invoked in order to
regulate and manage the situation before it developed further, and the complainants either left or were effectively discharged. Although the modern unit
did survive this crisis while Paddington did not, and the tensions in each were
resolved in different ways, neither institution created an environment in
which the more difficult manifestation of patients' distress could be
collectively contained and understood.

Crucial to Baron's critique of Paddington was that an abandonment of
rules and regulations in the name of democracy and the unchecked use of psychoanalysis (rather than enabling greater shared decision-making) actually
resulted in a situation in which psychoanalysis was used to pathologise and
control patients. For that reason, the next section explores the use of psychoanalysis in a modern TC context.

## Use of Psychoanalysis

In *Asylum to Anarchy* Baron (1987) argued that increasingly *all* of the actions of patients were interpreted in the light of their possible psychoanalytic psychopathology and this resulted in a totalising practice. In this respect, Baron compared her own analysis of Paddington with Goffman's highly in-fluential critique of mental hospitals in *Asylums* (1961). Goffman had high-lighted how mental hospitals operate as 'total institutions' in which all patients' behaviours are seen in the light of their social situation as mental patients, resulting in the use of dehumanising practices that ultimately attack the person's sense of self. Patients' behaviour is then therefore likely to be de-termined by an attempt to preserve a sense of selfhood in the context of being in a total institution. The tendency for psychoanalytic frameworks to result in totalising practices and conceptions can cause numerous problems such as in-dividualism, pathologisation and psychological reductionism. For example, it can result in the tendency to view individual patient's behaviour and thoughts as arising from particular institutionally sanctioned ideas about motives and pathologies. These are all examples of the continuous tension involved in any attempt to use psychoanalysis progressively (Gordon 2001). Furthermore, its use may be particularly problematic in TC environments, which by their very nature, incorporate more of the day-to-day lives of patients, especially in residential (but also in non-residential) environments.

One of the ways in which Paddington staff tried to work with the tension between psychoanalysis and democratisation was to use psychoanalysis as a way of understanding broader institutional dynamics and power structures. The idea at Paddington was that each individual could forge their own unique, personalised and unmediated relationship with the institution, which could then be examined and understood (Goodburn 1976). However, Baron's critique suggests that patients' responses and reactions were as much a reaction to the particular features of the day hospital itself as about revealing their particular personal psychodynamics. Baron's observation echoes Bion's critique of Ezriel's notion of the 'group transference', which was primarily conceived of in terms of its resonance among the life histories and internalised object relations of the members (which does not necessarily include wider social issues or the setting and social context itself). Bion argued that what Ezriel considered to be group transference might in fact be due to the experi-ence of being in a particular group situation, rather than necessarily being about individuals' assumed psychopathology (Ashbach and Shermer 1987).

Moreover, the predominantly psychoanalytic framework that Paddington staff used to understand the emerging situation, continued to thwart attempts to understand the individual's relationship with the institution and their

wider context. As we have seen, Goodburn felt in retrospect that a psychoanalytic understanding was often insufficient to understand the situation that
developed at Paddington because this was determined by a range of factors
that lay outside the day hospital's remit. For example, although Goodburn's
decision not to replace the cleaner could be viewed as an admirable attempt at
raising awareness about how oppresion operated as an important social
dynamic within the day hospital, ultimately the effects of this decision were
viewed primarily in psychoanalytic terms. Thus Goodburn reported that
patients who complained about nothing being done about the mess in the day
hospital were engaging in unconscious projection as they were really talking
about the rejected parts of their own personalities (Herbert 1976). Difficulties
in attempting a 'synthesis' between psychoanalysis and social theory, or trying
to maintain both in the absence of an adequate theory of the relationship
*between* them, usually results in psychoanalytic understanding taking
precedence.

Indeed, many Paddington patients complained about the overuse of psychoanalytic interpretation at the expense of other aspects of the community.
They argued that staff had already decided what was important and necessary,
despite having an explicit philosophy of democracy and shared decision-
making. This led to conflict over the locus of power and control in the
community as many felt that, despite espousing a philosophy of the equality
of collective group interpretation and the development of mutual enquiry,
the reality of community-led decision-making, patient participation and
self-organisation was illusory (Haddon 1979). Moreover, as one staff member
pointed out, this resulted in other potential action-orientated activities being
devalued:

> I always felt that psychoanalytic interpretations had a place in therapy if
> that is the therapy the users wanted, but they weren't useful in trying to
> organise anything, in fact they could be counter productive. It may well be
> because I am an OT and not a psychoanalyst, but I felt that the actions, be it
> crafts or politics, were practically empowering. I do believe in psychother-
> apy for personal insights [but] I felt as if the action side was belittled [at
> Paddington] and I believe this is at least partly why everything disinte-
> grated. (Lougher 2000)

However, again, rather than necessarily being a unique feature of Paddington, the lack of genuine patient and community decision-making and
social action is a frequent criticism of TCs, especially by ex-patients. For
example, it is argued that the circulation of notions about community
discussion and patients' participation mystifies the lack of real patient power

in decision-making (Brandon 1991; Chamberlain 1988). Such critiques argue that a pretence of shared decision-making is a smokescreen behind which real power still lies in the hands of psychiatric and/or psychoanalytic staff. It was this tacit psychoanalytic hierarchy, 'folded into the very texture of the day hospital', that prevented shared decision-making at Paddington (Oakley 1989, p.112). This important, but often overlooked, aspect of the critiques of Paddington highlights the possible over-reliance on psychoanalysis generally in TCs.

Despite attempts at increasing democratisation and shared decision-making, the ultimate authority in TCs is still almost invariably a medical psychiatric consultant who is also psychoanalytically trained. Kreeger warned that very few services have made real efforts to establish the genuine democratic principles of the TC approach. More specifically:

> All too often in a crisis situation staff abandon the principles of the TC and regress to a more orthodox, hierarchical position, in which their authority is used to control or remove the causative agent. In a sense it is easier to play the 'TC game' if the rules allow one to say 'I don't want to play anymore', when the going gets too difficult. (1970, p.149)

Similarly, Whiteley (1980) argued that whatever their professed allegiance to the therapeutic community ideology, insecure staff members tend to fall back on their traditional roles when under pressure from the patient group. More recent commentators have pointed out that, 'there is a well known, if rarely articulated, understanding that power ultimately rests upwards' (Winship and Haigh 1999, p.6). Indeed, even in the most 'democratised' TCs, in which some 'consultation' may be possible, it is questionable how much egalitarianism, enfranchisement and open communication are actually present within what is an ultimately closed system of decision-making (Winship and Haigh 1999). However, unlike at Paddington, while there are 'occasional crises of no-confidence', disquiet and opposition is now 'rarely expressed in more revolutionary terms' (Winship and Haigh 1999).

More radical efforts like Paddington, which tried to achieve greater egalitarianism, have often been dismissed as remnants of a utopian political past. Such attempts were criticised as colluding in an 'erosion of authority' or a 'denial of parentage' using a formulation in which we are asked to accept certain conventional, normative ideas about gender and parentage (Grunberg 1979). To deny or erode this parental authority is to invoke 'devilish forces' so what we must 'resurrect is the idea of the establishment of authority, of placing the King back on his throne' (Grunberg 1979, pp.9–10). As a result of these critiscisms, ideas about democratisation in TCs are actually of less consequence than before (Hinshelwood 1996; Winship and Haigh 1999) and, despite the proliferation of research about TCs, there has been little written about practices of democracy, decision-making and 'user involvement' in TCs.

This discussion highlights the problem of mental health practices that do not adequately explore the ideas of democratic processes beyond a therapeutic discourse. It seems that we can't necessarily assume links between therapeutic communities and democracy, nor take these links for granted in any simple way. TCs continue to privilege a therapeutic discourse that encompasses discursive frameworks relying upon psychoanalysis, individualisation and developmentalism rather than the processes and dynamics of democracy. We now, therefore, use the following section to review the possibilities for developing alternative frameworks of understandings in TCs.

## Alternative frameworks

Despite TCs 'commitment to the power of the community' (Tucker 2001, p.243) progressive ideas and concepts are often left assumed and undeveloped or merely reduced to their perceived psychodynamic origins and correlates. The historical reliance of TCs on charismatic leadership also feeds into the problems illustrated by accounts of the decline of TCs (Baron 1987; Hobson 1979). One problem with charismatic leadership is that, as well as a tendency to be necessarily fleeting and fragile, it is vulnerable to a totalising conception of practice (Melucci 1996). Looked at in this way, perhaps one of the lessons of Paddington should have been that decision-making in TCs should not ultimately be tied to psychoanalytic expertise that operates solely within a hierarchy of analytic knowledge and status (Haddon 1979).

In addition, while modern TCs may attend more to the social functioning of patients or community members than did earlier TCs, the 'ultimate' level of analysis still remains the individual or psychoanalytic subject. This can result in an understanding of the dynamics in a TC based on individual psychoanalysis alone, since this operates as the dominant hierarchy of meaning and explanation. Moreover, this prevents the possibility of developing alternative understandings. Many commentators pointed out that Paddington attempted to reproduce in the day hospital the blank screen of traditional one-to-one psychoanalysis, in part due to the influence of the work of Ezriel (Crocket 1978). It is worth reflecting on some of Ezriel's own words about the use of psychoanalysis. Although he did not 'for a moment consider that this strictly psychoanalytic technique is the only way of giving effective help to patients' (1950, p.59), he also took the view that 'none other than transference interpretations need be used' (1950, p.60). It is precisely this discrepancy that persists in TCs today. In other words, while there is an *outward* belief that psychoanalysis is not necessarily the most important influence in a TC, this does in fact simultaneously operate, in the last instance, as the most important, 'deepest' and privileged level of understanding.

In the modern unit, staff tried to resolve the tension between psychoanalysis and democratisation by viewing democratisation as being synonymous with therapy. Although staff were able to hold onto a variety of different understandings of the relationship between democratisation and psychotherapy, the dominant discourse in relation to shared decision-making frequently equated democracy or 'empowerment' with therapy itself, particularly within the specific TC structure and therapeutic model. This was frequently viewed as encompassing such things as the ability to listen and to be heard, negotiating, maintaining boundaries and supporting others. There existed a deep confusion and contradiction between user involvement as a therapeutic goal and the creation of opportunities for service users to significantly influence the nature of support/therapy and the ways these services are informed. Indeed, compared with the influence of the setting and the staff, patients exert their influence on the way a TC is run in a relatively passive way, involving a 'willingness to co-operate, to participate, to accept the staff's philosophy' (Kennard 1979, p.190).

This belief that the essence of TC practice is based upon empowerment frequently functions to prevent those running TCs from seeing beyond a narrowly defined interpersonal view of empowerment, however important that may be. For example, Sharp (1975) criticised the consensual view of the democratic process that operates in TCs as functioning to prevent the intrusion of wider conceptions of democracy. Moreover, this consensual view results in a tendency to reduce empowerment to an individual attribute and emphasise clients' abilities to do social and/or occupational tasks to fit into an 'already given, uncontested social world' (McLean 1995, p.1057).

However, I would argue that the importance of 'democracy' lies in its potential to facilitate the expression of structural difficulties and complaints without recourse to pathologisation. Patient perspectives are a necessary condition for the establishment of transformative social relations. Democracy therefore has benefits beyond the psychological ones for their members, including the power to define and contest 'mental health' or 'illness' itself (Barnes and Bowl 2001). Greater democracy in psychiatry allows for the collective will and needs of patients to be articulated. Over recent years survivors' views on experiences such as hearing voices (Coleman and Smith 1997; Downs 2001; McLaughlin 2000; Romme and Escher 2000) and self-harm (Babiker and Arnold 1997; Cresswell 2004; Pembroke 1998) have facilitated greater professional understanding as well as viable self-help movements and strategies. Unfortunately, one of the effects of the continued dominance of psychoanalytic thinking in TCs is the development of increasingly internalised and inward-looking practices. This can cut TCs off from wider progressive initiatives within and beyond mental health (Coppock and Hopton 2000; Newnes, Holmes and Dunn 1999, 2001; Parker *et al.* 1995).

Thus, tying democratisation too closely to patient improvement and therapy can limit the creative potential of patient participation, and reduce it to paternalistic considerations of patients' 'best interests' (Barnes and Bowl 2001). If fuller participation and wider influence is not viewed as important in its own right, this will inevitably result in the blunting of the potential critical edge of notions of involvement and empowerment. This situation can result in a privileging of individualised and psychologised interventions. Furthermore, if participation is viewed primarily as a technique or instrument in the service of individual therapy, this may serve only to enforce participation on community members, however subtly achieved. In this way greater 'involvement' may always have a tendency to result in greater compliance with explicit and implicit regulative practices. Baron clearly indicated this in relation to Paddington, but this discussion suggests her point should be read as being more widely applicable:

> While patient participation was indeed encouraged, it is an ironical fact that the more therapeutic and less custodial the institution, the more the staff tend to impress on the patient that he is ill and that the trouble lies within himself: he must change his conception of himself and start relating to people differently. (1987, p.144)

Baron's critique also suggested that the Paddington crisis emerged because concrete material and psychodynamic issues were not kept distinct and separate, as there were no separate meetings whereby conscious practical matters were decided without exploration of their unconscious meaning. Therefore, in one article she argued that if only they had preserved separate community meetings Paddington 'might still be flourishing'.

> The intrusive control of patients would be limited if a context were provided where the everyday as opposed to unconscious meaning of patients' statements could be seen as valid…illegitimately reductive explanations should be avoided in this context. (Baron 1984b, p.169)

In general, regular community meetings are seen as vital for the discussion of organisational matters in TCs. However in most TCs, while practical matters and unconscious motives are theoretically kept separate, this is never straightforward and is part of an ongoing struggle. What is considered to be a 'reasonable' practical matter is always open to interpretation and contestation. In addition, community meetings have simultaneously been described as the main site for the exercise of peer and community control or, alternatively, as manipulation of patients in a TC (Manning 1989). In this regard, it is relevant to note that in the modern unit's community meetings there was little time available for critical open discussion as these were usually filled up with staff (and patients') agenda items about individual patients.

In the modern unit it was a patients' committee meeting, rather than the community meeting, that operated as the only forum explicitly working with patients' concrete, ongoing concerns on their own terms. This meeting included representation from the patient group and the staff team. However, while it did function as a useful and unique place in the community, it did not necessarily enable patients' concerns and difficulties with its structure to be adequately addressed. Although patients did feel that it was a refreshing space in which to be heard, and to have a more equal dialogue, change was nevertheless extremely slow – and, indeed, they questioned whether any real meaningful change was in fact possible. This was partly due to wider institutional constraints such as resources, bureaucracies and safety or risk procedures, and yet could also be attributed to patients' concerns later being re-framed psychoanalytically in staff meetings. Furthermore, it was always possible to override any decisions made in the committee meetings. Indeed, when a number of patients complained and the atmosphere was difficult in the modern unit, staff actually cancelled the meeting.

The continued absence of any alternative collective frameworks to psychoanalysis through which to understand community dynamics in TCs can contribute to irrevocable splits, polarisations and complaints. Although some people have advocated the further development and integration of psychodynamics and group analysis as a way through these difficulties (Winship 1995, 1997; Winship and Pines 1996), I would argue instead for the necessity of developing alternative non-psychoanalytic and non-familial community and group frameworks and concepts.

Mainstream psychology and psychoanalysis tends to view people as isolated individuals rather than members of specific social and cultural practices (Burman 1994, 1996). Therefore, if the nature of the 'individual' in the TC is construed primarily as a psychoanalytic subject, this constructs not an active, social-political-cultural subject, but a 'responsible', pathologised and irrational one. Psychoanalytic discourse relies upon conventional notions of the family and TCs are no exception. TCs often explicitly utilise notions of the community as merely an extended family and assume that the conventional family unit should be invoked as the primary mode of therapeutic under-standing. In this way familial concepts are readily drawn upon when viewing events such as cleaning, cooking, eating and living arrangements in TCs. This is also evident in ways in which the community itself is viewed as a familial structure, in which the consultant is often referred to as the head of the com-munity family.

The dominance of prevailing notions of democracy, the family and gender (Adorno et al. 1982) makes the development of alternative frameworks for understanding community dynamics difficult to generate. In addition, given the ways in which broader practices of liberal democracy have been tied to particular (bourgeois, middle-class and heterosexual) familial dynamics and relations, especially mothering (Walkerdine and Lucey 1989), it is perhaps not surprising that psychoanalytic approaches, including TCs, also subscribe to such explanations.

In addition, while a familial framework could introduce alternative notions – for example, of siblings acknowledging their shared positions – psychoanalytic discourse tends to focus more readily on sibling 'rivalry' rather than on solidarity. Moreover, this can function to actively pathologise patients who adopt alternative positions in the community that challenge, or stand outside, these formulations and assumptions. For example, in the modern unit it was notable that a couple of patients attempted to adopt the position of an 'advocate' in relation to the patient who was being discharged. However, it was difficult for staff to view this position as positive within their dominant framework, and consequently, it was viewed as further evidence for individu-ally ascribed difficulties in therapy.

Furthermore, because the meanings ascribed to individual and commu-nity dynamics in TCs are developed from psychoanalysis, their framework is limited in terms of developing an understanding of the social. Because this model is primarily child-focused, it is frequently dyadic and this prevents the facilitation of alternative community- or group-specific formulations, struc-tures and possibilities (Burman 2001; Dalal 1998; Mitchell 1988). Such dyadic frameworks are of limited value in conceptualising community rela-tions which may require more diverse, malleable and group- or commu-nity-specific forms (Burman 2001; Dalal 1998; Davison 2001). Indeed, the fact that Western societies conceive of 'mental health' as an individual attrib-ute (however poorly defined), rather than as a property of groups or commu-nities (Bondi and Burman 2001), indicates how difficult it might be to develop group, let alone community-specific, concepts in mental health ser-vices. However, if TCs are really to develop as a socio-political, commu-nity-based approach (Tucker 2000), it is necessary to find ways of breaking out of this circularity in order to offer more alternative and progressive frameworks.

Of course, the critique that TCs have not effectively utilised social theories and that they rely too heavily on psychodynamic and group-analytic concepts is not new. Many social researchers have drawn attention to this difficulty (Chapman 1986, 1988; Haddon 1979; Lees and Manning 1984; Manning 1989; Sharp 1975). For example, Manning (1989) urged TCs to utilise and develop modern social theories in order to revitalise the radical potential of the therapeutic community, which has been overshadowed and eclipsed by group psychotherapy. However, the 'unacknowledged' over-emphasis on psychodynamics at the expense of social theory is still apparent and problematic both within TCs and group analysis (Craib 2001; Dalal 1998).

Thus the theory and practice of group analysis, despite its focus on 'the group' remains wedded to its psychoanalytic roots (Carter 2001; Dalal 1998). Dalal (1998) argues that group analysis requires real group-specific constructs and the evolution of a new language to conceive thoroughly of the group and the social – and by the group he doesn't just mean the group analytic abstraction. Dalal's appeal to 'take the group seriously' entails an understanding of the social construction of all groups and the social configurations of power relations from which both the individual and group emerge. In other words, group analysis has not produced a theory that is truly 'group analytic' (Carter 2001). More than this, others have highlighted the 'one-way traffic' between group analysis and TCs such that group analysts often provide expertise and commentary on TCs, but rarely is there any evidence of a TC perspective being applied to group analysis (Davison 2001). Indeed, applying the logic of Dalal and Carter's argument, there is perhaps no TC perspective that takes 'the community' seriously, either in terms of its ideology of shared decision-making, a culture of open enquiry or patient collective empowerment.

While the notion of a 'culture of enquiry' is a useful and important concept in the formulation of TC principles and practice (Main 1983; Norton 1996), it is an under-theorised and underdeveloped concept in TCs. In essence, it refers to the possibility that anything and everything in the community can be talked about, commented upon, questioned or challenged. More recently, it has been referred to more loosely as 'openness' and has been used to refer to the opportunities to challenge decisions, power and authority (Haigh 1999). The preservation and maintenance of this culture of enquiry is deemed crucial for both the therapeutic and democratic values at the centre of TC practice. However, despite this, dealing with patients' challenges and critiques continues to be problematic because the principle of a culture of enquiry is constrained by the particular psychotherapeutic model used to

inform the nature of democratisation. For example, what staff in both Paddington and the modern unit deemed necessary for a satisfactory 'therapeutic'
enquiry ensured that any 'critical enquiry' did not extend to challenging the
very (psychotherapeutic) model against which this notion had been defined.

TCs inevitably operate at the edge of a number of related contradictions.
These include the tension between providing an environment whereby patients can learn to live in the 'real world' and the development of an 'ideal culture' (Manning 1979, p.294). Other contradictions include the tension
between operating as a professional intervention as opposed to the development of patients as therapists, and the tension between individual freedom
and effective social organisation (Kennard 1982). Indeed, the 'working
through' of contradictory phenomena has been viewed as an important part
of the therapeutic process in TCs (Bloor 1981). However, this approach often
misses the social reality of these conflicts, as well as how such contradictions
can open up possibilities of resistance (Sharp 1975). The lack of sufficient attention to these contradictions was highlighted in Rapoport's classic study of
a TC (1960). Rapoport's study is frequently referred to in the modern TC literature due to his identification of the often quoted TC principles of democracy, permissiveness, communalism and reality confrontation. However, the
important observations that he also made about the inherent contradictions in
implementing these principles has rarely been referred to, nor addressed
(Manning 1989).

## Paradoxical spaces

To become more aware of ongoing conflicts inherent in TC practices requires
open and critical reflection about the consequences of our current strategies
for engaging with paradox. The development of a non-psychoanalytic,
reflexive approach may offset the problem of individual psychologisation,
de-politicisation and the pathologisation of structural contradictions and
paradoxes. To avoid these problems I have used the term 'paradox', rather than
the prevailing psychoanalytic notions of 'conflict' and 'ambivalence'. All too
often premature resolutions are imposed upon a situation in which conflicts
have been activated because they are not conceivable within the current
discourse of possibilities used to frame the situation. By making the current
forms of resolution of paradoxes more explicit, it is possible to become more
aware of the possibility of alternative, more creative and open-minded strategies of engaging with conflict (Dunford and Palmer 1998; Grant, Keenoy and
Oswick 1998; Rappaport 1986).

Through ongoing, reflective and critical practice, generated through the elaboration of specific but shared spaces for discussions, it may be possible to accept and work with the reality of patients' complaints and demands. It is the interaction and exploration of different perspectives in TCs that could produce more productive dialogue and negotiation. If the maintenance of a culture of enquiry depends not on particular structures, but upon the culture engendered to facilitate communication (Norton 1996), then the provision of specific spaces in TCs must develop alongside a more fundamental shift in the prevalence of totalising (predominantly psychoanalytic) discourses and frameworks.

The idea of what are called 'paradoxical spaces' developed in feminist geography can be helpful here (Rose 1993). Consciousness of the dynamic tensions within such spaces allows for the articulation of difference as well as the creative expression of the 'troubled relation' between paradoxes (p.159). Attempts to forge such diffused paradoxical spaces might attune us to the possibilities and potentials of working creatively with paradoxes, rather than seeking their one-sided resolution (Rappaport 1986). This 'doubled vision' (Rose 1993) simultaneously accepts the different expressions of paradox and allows for their fuller understanding.

In this way, 'threats' or challenges from the patient group can be seen not as problems to be overcome but as expressions of important paradoxes in the relationship between patients, the TC and the social context. The ability to develop an openness to challenge and the possibility of alternative perspectives could be creative and transformatory:

> It is that which is new or unexpected, that which shocks, surprises us, takes us aback, challenges our beliefs, and threatens us with transformation... The other is not simply what we make of it, what we take it to be. It is also that which resists, eludes, goes beyond our reading of it, and is able to affect us in turn. (Falzon 1998, pp.89–94)

However, the maintenance of a culture of enquiry and the forging of paradoxical spaces are notoriously difficult and problematic goals. For example, paradoxical spaces do not come 'naturally' and neither are they inherently radical or subversive (Rose 1993). They are historically and locally specific, partial and strategic. To make this a concrete possibility, it is necessary to look towards progressive and alternative community formulations and wider cultural and political resources and practices (Glennister 2002; Hopton 2000). It is this rather than psychoanalysis which might extend the democratic and emancipatory values that have inspired so many in the TC movement.

The ability of Paddington to operate as a 'site of convergence' for progressive social forces during the early 1970s was linked to the wider political framework and context within which its members actively participated. For a brief time during the early 1970s Paddington did relate its psychoanalytic thinking to a broader social movement and growing political awareness. This enabled the 'working through' of transference relationships to be broadened out beyond familial parent–child relations and in turn opened up other possibilities for social relationships of a different kind.

In summary, rather than being an example of 'bad' TC practice, the story of Paddington actually exposes some of the more profound difficulties and paradoxes within TCs between democratisation and the use of psychoanalysis. These problems and ongoing tensions do not necessarily mean such endeavours are always doomed to failure. Rather than offer any final answers or solutions, I have highlighted key consequences of the ways in which these problems have been posed and resolved in a modern TC. It remains unclear whether these paradoxes mean that TCs are ultimately flawed, or whether they can be an important space in which such paradoxes may be revealed and reflected upon. Indeed, the necessity of TCs working with these contradictions has been described as the 'essential challenge' of TCs which 'can only be resolved from moment to moment and cannot go out of date' (Kennard 1982, p.175). However, this discussion has aimed to illustrate how these fundamental conflicts cannot, and should not, be reduced to individual psychological and therapeutic concerns alone.

# CHAPTER NINE

# Asylum to Action

## Beyond the Therapeutic Community

There can be no definitive history of Paddington Day Hospital; all accounts are partial and situated and the differing interpretations of the events at Paddington merely serve to illustrate this. However, although its complex story resists easy analysis, most accounts have been 'monological' in that they tend towards a reasoned closure of interpretations. In this way they have functioned like a consumable pill of history: an easily digestible story providing symptomatic, but insubstantial, relief. In my account, however, I have striven to produce a struggle-based dialogical account that prioritises processes of contestation, paradox and indeterminacy (Keenoy, Oswick and Grant 1997).

Claims to 'historical truth' frequently foreclose the field of current action and constrain future possibilities. Histories are not simple representations of the past, but 'practically orientated attempts to reshape our effective collective understandings of the past' (Norman 1998, p.162). The production of counter discourses and narratives about historical events can 'change the rules' of what is possible and necessary (Venn 1992). Furthermore:

> There is a 'field' of overlapping narratives that shape a society's awareness of its historical situation. This consciousness is 'effective' because it orients us practically. The historian, through research and storytelling, can help to reshape this field, and in so doing alter the field of possibilities we confront, both individually and as a society. (Norman 1998, p.170)

In re-writing the story of Paddington I have tried to challenge dominant thinking and expand the realms of possibility. My hope is that this will renew some of the radical aspirations that have galvanised the TC movement over the years, since, unfortunately, many of these more radical initiatives have been pathologised and demonised. What are frequently remembered about such initiatives are examples of supposed extremism, regression or moral degradation, rather than some of their important innovations. For example, the image of Mary Barnes smearing her own faeces over the walls remains the

most commonly recalled version of Kingsley Hall as a whole, despite the
many positive aspects of her 'recovery' and the flourishing of her artistic creativity in this libertarian context (Barnes and Scott 1989).

## Post-psychiatry

Rather than merely being a story of 'asylum to anarchy', I believe that the
lessons of Paddington, both its successes and failures, could play an important
role in the history of the development of radical psychiatric initiatives. For a
brief moment, Paddington provided a setting that engendered and prefigured
the pioneering social relations necessary for the development of innovative
services (Burton 2000). Such social settings, whether or not they are considered a success or failure, are important for the moments at which they were
'prefigurative' – releasing new learning about social relations, challenging
perceptions and practices and benefiting many who participated. Yet Paddington is also another example of the complexities inherent in the desire to
develop a more egalitarian social setting in which the experience of madness
and distress could be both expressed and understood in relation to its social
context. Although such ambitions were never going to be easy to achieve,
attempts at doing so deserve serious appraisal.

In addition, Paddington played an important part in the history of the
patients' movement, the TC movement and the anti-psychiatry movement
and, even more importantly, focused attention on the points at which these
converged. And yet, it does not comfortably insert itself into the history of
these movements in any clear and unambiguous way. In particular, while the
story of Paddington highlights the relationship between TCs and the
emergence of the modern patients' movement through the formation of the
MPU, this relationship was never straightforward. This lack of a 'fit' is echoed
in modern TCs, where the relationship between TCs and the service users'
movement continues to be fraught and littered with tensions.

In order to continue to be part of a challenging movement of 'post-psychiatry' (Bracken and Thomas 2001, 2005), TCs need to operate as both a
'convergent space' (Routledge 2001) for progressive social forces, and also as
a conscious 'paradoxical space' (Rose 1993) when difficulties and dilemmas
inevitably arise. Paddington was able to be a convergent space in the early
1970s, inspiring social action and the MPU. However, like many modern
TCs, it failed to offer a paradoxical space in which the tensions within and
beyond the TC could be revealed, understood and acted upon.

Part of the success of initiatives like Soteria House in the USA and the
Italian democratic psychiatry movement was their refusal to adhere to thera-

peutic orthodoxy. Such projects embraced a range of theoretical ideas that included, but were not confined to, psychotherapeutic and psychoanalytic frameworks. Inspired by Kingsley Hall in East London in the 1960s, Mosher and his colleagues set up a libertarian, yet safe, home-like environment whereby people could be supported to go through a 'psychotic' experience without recourse to medication or hospitalisation. Like Kingsley Hall and Paddington, but unlike many contemporary TCs, Soteria House moved away from pre-set community schedules in favour of individuals being able to find and develop their own structures and rules appropriate to their needs (which should be open to negotiation) (Mosher 1991a, b). Although limited medication was sometimes used sparingly and some ideas from psychoanalysis were drawn upon, it was neither of these that primarily guided intervention.

Soteria House explicitly tried to avoid imposing a particular psychological model such as psychoanalysis and instead tried to encourage people to find their own ways of understanding their experience. Other theoretical influences came from existentialism, phenomenology, anti-psychiatry, and patients' perspectives as well as psychoanalysis (Mosher *et al.* 2004). Any approach that believes it has access to the 'truth' or the solution to madness and distress is bound to encounter difficulties. Inherent in the idea of 'post-psychiatry' is the embracing of multiple and diverse perspectives and approaches that take full account of the wider social context out of which distress inevitably arises (Bracken and Thomas 2001, 2005).

Ultimately, Paddington fell short of this, not because of its libertarian or radical tendencies but because it fell into a mistaken belief in the primacy of psychoanalysis as the key to understanding. During the period of social action at Paddington, psychoanalytic understandings nestled amongst, and were nourished by, other social and political approaches and understandings. However, the gradual severance of its connection with a wider cultural climate and other progressive ideas resulted in its psychoanalytic approach being more reactive than proactive and progressive.

Unfortunately, the demise of Paddington corresponded with a decline in TCs as part of an ambitious project of social change within and beyond psychiatry. We have witnessed a similar fate in the development of psychoanalysis, which suffered from a repression of its original, more radical, aspirations (Jacoby 1983). Jacoby has argued that this decline is synonymous with the repression of classical psychoanalysis itself. Whether there is a radical 'core' to either psychoanalysis or TCs remains an open question. Kennard has argued that there is something inherently progressive about TCs because they embody certain socially minded ideas and impulses (Kennard 1991). Nevertheless, TCs have in common with psychoanalysis a tendency to be paradoxical in their claims to radicalism as they operate within a contradictory political and cultural landscape, resulting in both a reinforcement of, and resistance to, prevailing ideologies (Parker 1997).

Precisely because of this, it is necessary to retrieve a sense of the radical spirit that could inspire the TC movement to move beyond the limitations of its current conception. Despite many elements of progress in the delivery of mental health services, the current context serves to squeeze out the possibilities for developing more radical conceptualisations of TC practice, as the next section will argue.

## Current context

The period between the demise of Paddington and the development of current TC practices witnessed a number of conflicting social, economic and political changes. The existence of therapeutic communities has increasingly come under threat from funders influenced by a number of factors. Most obviously, financial pressures have limited the extent of investment in TCs, but wider ideological forces have also placed limitations on their development. Unfortunately, the need to protect the existence of TCs in a hostile context resulted in attempts to restore faith in already existing TC models of practice. The desire to become a part of mainstream psychiatry included a 'trade off', which often resulted in greater adherence to strict procedures and regulations rather than an open and rigorous critical enquiry into its own models and theories of practice.

More notably, this period has seen the rise of two seemingly conflicting political forces which have sometimes converged and resulted in a lessened interest in TCs. On the one hand, a conservative political climate under the Thatcher government involved attacks on the Welfare State in general and on ideas of collectivism, a central notion in TCs (Winship 1995; Winship and Haigh 2000). On the other hand, as the rights-based welfare users' movement has grown more individualised, user-defined alternatives have been developed and advocated, sometimes at the expense of TCs.

The two forces of the user movement and the new right have come together through the ideas of consumerism and individual choice, both of which have been promoted by Thatcherism and embraced by the New Labour government. The kind of consequences of this development can perhaps be seen in the fate of Paddington Day Hospital. The crisis at Paddington can be viewed as highlighting a key moment in history of the NHS and welfare services when communalism and collective decision-making gave way to an increasingly individualist consumerist ideology. However, although the growth of notions of 'consumer choice' provides some leverage for the growing service users' movement, it may ultimately constrain and limit its wider impact in terms of generating innovative collective practices.

In a contemporary context, while the adoption of the principles and practices of community care and individualised care budgets (or direct payments) can offer opportunities for more user-defined alternatives, they don't necessarily promote collective service provision or communalism. Current service developments and priorities and agendas such as 'social inclusion' do not help evolve new and specialised services able to respond to the changing and dynamic needs of groups and communities, rather than just individuals (Spandler 2004).

Another related change that has occurred since the events at Paddington has been the development of concepts and practices of efficiency, accountability and managerialism (Parton 2003). Concerns about standardising practice to ensure that professionals work according to certain sanctioned rules and procedures mean that work has had to be monitored, justified and accountable. Inquiries have played some part in this scenario by encouraging greater proceduralism and the solidification of hierarchialism. While inquiries into the functioning of projects like Paddington could have opened up debate about some of the conflicts and paradoxes addressed here, they have more often promoted conservatism, anxiety and defensive practices instead (Stanley and Manthorpe 2004). In addition, simultaneous attacks on the public-sector workforce and trade unionism has led to an increase in managerialism, which prioritises efficiency, value for money and performance rather than experimentation and innovation.

Much of this is not new. Many alternative psychiatry initiatives have not been tolerated, developed or invested in because ultimately they were seen to contradict the perceived grounds of moral acceptability of the time. Although Wilfred Bion's pioneering post-war work with traumatised soldiers at Northfield Hospital in Birmingham is now the stuff of legend it was in fact prematurely cut short after only six weeks because the military authorities feared that it would lead to anarchy and chaos (Bridger 1985; Main 1983). David Cooper's more radical and anti-psychiatric pioneering work with young men diagnosed with schizophrenia at Villa 21 in Shenley Hospital (Cooper 1965, 1967) aroused similar concerns about cleanliness, indiscipline and the extent of patient responsibility (Kennard 1998; Pullen 1999). Castel et al. (1982) listed numerous examples of health departments enforcing health and safety regulations against alternative free clinics in the USA, insisting on medical cover, as well as certain levels of cleanliness. They convincingly illustrated how the pressure of external forces to conform to pre-set standards results in the co-option, medicalisation and psychiatrisation of alternative mental health initiatives.

Recent years have seen a marked increase in external demands that mental health services incorporate more structures, assessments and other formalised regulations and procedures. Inevitably this has infected the TC movement, leading to recent moves to greater regulation and professionalisation, and functions that suffocate any radical potential left in TCs (Cooper 1999). While these imperatives are strongest in the statutory sector and the NHS in particular, independent or voluntary sector organisations are also increasingly forced to comply with particular external regulations in order to secure ongoing funding (Berke 2003).

Again, although risk avoidance has been a key factor in mental health services for some time, recent years have witnessed concerns over 'risk' becoming increasingly the key concern in the mental health field and beyond (Castel 1991; Furedi 1997; Rose 1996). The need to avoid 'danger' and harm has led to discourses and practices of risk aversion and management and these have developed to such a degree that health and welfare professionals are increasingly seen as 'risk managers' (Davis 1996). Furthermore, public debates, policies and mental health practices have been influenced, if not defined, by a media preoccupation with issues of safety (Szmukler and Holloway 2000). This renders risk-taking itself as a dangerous activity and, in turn, prevents a more positive view of risk-taking as opening up opportunities to take chances in order to enable greater change.

This risk-avoidant culture functions to produce radical experimentation as problematic and dangerous. It also limits the ability of TCs to take the risks necessary to provide the conditions through which people can 'escape from the intra-psychic, inter personal and bio-chemical straight jackets in which they had been imprisoned, or in which they had imprisoned themselves' (Berke 2003, p.3). Cooper (2001) describes our collectively developed and reproduced irrational anxieties around risk, resulting in our collusion in demands for greater regulation and management and the corresponding threat to potential creativity and authenticity in welfare practices. By institutionalising caution, the precautionary principle imposes a doctrine of limits. It offers security, but in exchange for lowering expectations, limiting growth and preventing experimentation and change.

Another wider factor that figures in the current context is the continuing rise of 'evidence-based practice' (Gibbs and Gambrill 2002; Harrison 1998; Pope 2003). The potential of many libertarian and radical initiatives has, by their very nature, been hard to assess and evaluate. Despite this, the neglect of serious attention to such developments cannot simply be due to a lack of evidence. Research that demonstrated the positive long-term outcomes for residents of Soteria House compared with conventional in-patient treatment testifies to this (Bola and Mosher 2003; Mosher 1999; Mosher *et al.* 2004). Despite such favourable outcomes, risk avoidance usually overrides the possibility of investing in such alternatives and often plays a more crucial role than 'evidence' as such (Cooper 2003).

Yet another crucial limiting factor to the development of radical therapeutic communities has been the continued dominance of the bio-chemical model of psychiatry. Despite evidence from the World Health Organisation that there is little correlation between use of neuroleptic medication and 'recovery from schizophrenia' (Jablensky 1992; Leff 1992; Warner 1994), the pervasive influence of the pharmaceutical industry over the treatment of mental distress continues (Moncrieff, Hopker and Thomas 2005). In this context the possibilities for extending and tolerating the expression of madness and disturbance without conventional bio-chemical intervention are often closed off in mainstream psychiatry (Burston 1996; Mosher 1991a, b).

What was crucial in enabling the development of non-medical, anti-psychiatry alternatives was the radical climate during the late 1960s. Another key factor in the relative success of Soteria House and the Italian reforms was their awareness of and attention to wider social structures, networks and support. It follows that another important limiting factor in the current climate is the lack of a wider supportive counter-culture that could help nourish alternative ideas and sustain critical and radical communities. Indeed, the ability to develop and maintain the TC movement as a critical and progressive force within psychiatry is enhanced (or limited) by its connection to wider progressive social forces and, specifically, progressive social movements.

Consequently, the prevailing conditions of political possibility have limited conceptions and practice in TCs and constrained the opportunities for TCs to continue and expand their more radical tradition. This current context ensures that events and practices like Paddington are unlikely to be repeated and that some of the more fundamental difficulties and conflicts that occurred here will remain un-addressed in more conventional TC practices.

## Therapeutic Communities today and beyond

Since Paddington, the development of other alternatives on the margins of psychiatry – not least from patients and survivors themselves – has somewhat eclipsed TCs as the progressive alternative in psychiatry (Brandon 1991; Hopton 2000). Such developments have outdated Maxwell Jones' assertion that 'the concept of a Therapeutic Community carries the idea of the patient's self-determination to a new stage' (Jones 1968, p.43). In this context, it is doubtful whether TCs can continue to claim their status as the 'only branch of psychiatry, to date, that has an explicit historical interest in democracy' (Winship and Haigh 2000, p.53). Despite such declarations, TCs have come up with remarkably few alternative forms of democracy, that do not just mirror and reproduce wider liberal democratic and non-democratic forces. It is perhaps ironic that TCs, despite being based upon notions of community and democracy, have yet to develop alternative, progressive practices of either.

Furthermore, in part as a consequence of being forced into a project of survival, TCs have become more increasingly de-cultured, professionalised and streamlined (Cooper 1999). This has partly arisen due to a current context that has created a new social space for the TC as a specialised treatment regime for people labelled as 'personality disordered'. The corresponding focus of TCs on personality disorder has been described as both the greatest strength and the greatest weakness of the current TC movement (Hopton 2001). On the one hand, it represents a more progressive end of the treatment of personality disorders, which are thus viewed not merely as 'badness' but as a treatable and even reasonable reaction to intolerable early experiences of physical, emotional and/or sexual abuse and neglect. In this way, the new focus might lead to more sensitive treatment than might result from recent government proposals to introduce more compulsory treatment in the community. Fundamental principles of TCs include that TC membership should be voluntary and the idea that distress and psychosocial pathology should be understood as arising from particular social and familial circumstances rather than merely medicated away or 'controlled'. Yet, on the other hand, this application of TCs simultaneously reinforces the concept of personality disorder itself as an illness requiring specialised treatment and containment by experts.

A growing critique of the concept and function of personality disorder itself from researchers, feminists and service users (Asylum 2004; Castillo 2000; Nehls 1999; Pilgrim 2001) may bring us back to one of the historical functions of TCs: a technique for the normalisation, social regulation and the governance of selves (Rose 1986). In this context it could be argued that TCs are in danger of becoming merely a reprogramming device designed to 'drive home the stringent rules that are supposed to govern normal existence' (Castel *et al.* 1982, p.194).

In this way, TCs could become formalised procedures for re-sealing the separation, or 'fall out', between individuals and their social context through the promotion of self-regulation and responsibility, the development of internalised controls, peer monitoring and regulation. Viewed like this, rather than as a radical social and political initiative, therapeutic communities merely 'provide a therapeutic rationale for the containment of those sectors who are, in one way or another, resistant to its techniques of normalisation' (Rose 1986, p.77). Currently these may include persistent self-harmers, the repetitively suicidal, the anti-social, and people who resist being 'socially included' and involved in the structures of mainstream society.

This complication illustrates the limitation of focusing on the development of TCs as the key solution to the ongoing problem of how we collectively respond to individually ascribed 'madness' or deviance within wider structures of power, inequality and exclusion. The Italian radical psychiatrist Franco Basaglia, a key theorist in the Italian democratic psychiatry movement, had a unique perspective on TCs which is worth reflecting on here. According to Basaglia, the therapeutic community should never become a new technical model of treating madness but should create the conditions in which the institution itself is negated and transcended. He warns us that despite being developed from a desire to challenge the conventional mental hospital, TCs could themselves become just another fossilised model of treatment. Therefore, 'as a safeguard against their becoming an element of oppression themselves, [they should] be constantly reverting to reality to reinvigorate the spirit of renewal that originally informed them' (Basaglia 1985, p.42). Basaglia (1987) argues that while TCs were important this was only as the first step in a long process of radical change and they should be seen as a transitional point in a longer dynamic of innovation, change and struggle. He argues that the continual challenge of social conflicts, the articulation of new needs, and the dynamics of inclusion and exclusion may begin with the therapeutic community but must progress through new forms of struggle.

> The therapeutic community may be considered to have been a necessary step in the evolution of the mental hospital... but it cannot be regarded as the ultimate goal. It was a transitory phase, a holding action, until the situation itself evolved, bringing us new insights. What is important for the moment is that we should be able to maintain, confront, and accept our contradictions without yielding to the temptation to run away from and thus deny them. (Basaglia 1985, p.50)

Advocating specific, concrete alternatives has always been a tension in radical mental health movements, particularly as they have a tendency to uncritically adopt standardised, dominant therapeutic techniques and frameworks such as psychoanalysis (Brandon 1991; Castel et al. 1982; Coppock and Hopton 2000; Papeschi 1985; Parker et al. 1995). Practices constituted as 'alternatives' too readily end up mirroring the problems they were attempting to address because they are so heavily marked by what they oppose (Parker et al.

1995, p.36). Progressive psychiatric innovation can only proceed through continual crises and self-criticism or by dialectical supercession, which prevents any premature closure or crystallisation of change into new immobile institutions, even if these may seem more modern, efficient or 'democratic' (Donnelly 1992). Mike Lawson (1999), who was specifically reflecting upon his experiences at Paddington, articulated a similar critique:

> from the frying pan into the fire... there's a danger of, if the shift goes from what we have now which is primarily biological psychiatry to social psychiatry, it's just going to be like the move from Napsbury [a conventional asylum] to Paddington Day Hospital... That isn't where the dynamic comes from, it comes from those people who are doing the protest and it still does... Unless the power is in the hands of the person who's being done, what happens all too readily and easily is the power gets transferred to another set of oppressions against the individual, so we never get to play with the ball.

Such critiques provide an important cautionary analysis, particularly in the context of modern developments in TC theory and practice. Changes in TC practices seem to have confirmed Basaglia's fears that the therapeutic community movement has shifted from a social movement to an established professional therapeutic model of intervention (Kennard 1986). Manning (1989) foresaw this development and referred to it as 'routinisation'. These changes include such things as the increasing internal specialisation and selection of patients and accredited training of staff in order to be maximally effective rather than experimental. The following quote illustrates how, in an effort to afford TCs status and survival, they have moved from being a responsive 'movement' to a clearly defined treatment 'model':

> Once there was a TC movement; then there was a TC method; and now we have TC maxim – an axiom; a self-evident proposition... There is room for fine tuning in TCs (always), but now we know what works best and for whom. (Winship 2001, p.10)

The arguments presented here suggest that, rather than assuming that TCs have attained theoretical development and coherence, they are actually steeped in confusion, conflict and ambiguity like group psychotherapies in general (Haigh 2004; Nitsun 1996). Too frequently, received professional wisdom can become unchallengeable rules and 'facts', resulting in regulations and structures that appear self-evident and necessary. It is the taking up of totalising positions on the dilemmas and paradoxes that are inherent to TCs that can become over-predictive and standardised, concealing our necessary ongoing and profound uncertainty. Yet, like many initiatives, the grounds of TC knowledge is insecure, unstable, shifting, uncertain and, most importantly, contested. The challenge posed by the so called 'mentally ill' – the need to be 'therapeutic' yet to also accept and facilitate patients' own self-organisation and critiques – exposes the problem that faces mental health services generally, not just TCs.

A struggle for greater democracy neither surrenders itself to its illusions, nor aspires to a permanent substitute (Esteva 1999). This means developing spaces that enable greater democratic dialogue such that our aim is to struggle to 'widen, strengthen and deepen the space where people can exert their own power' (p.154). Therefore, while it remains important to develop specific therapeutic communities of safety, exploration and freedom, it is perhaps more important to maintain and cultivate the radical spirit necessary to enable the creation of wider critical communities and 'cultures of enquiry' both within and beyond TCs.

It remains to be seen whether TCs will ever be able to revisit some of the more challenging questions that the practice of Paddington posed but was unable to resolve. The theoretical resources and alternative narratives outlined here might help to elaborate how to move beyond narrowly defined therapeutic communities and uses of psychoanalytic expertise when opportunities for social change arise through critical attention to moments of paradox. What continues to remain untheorised – and, frequently, unpractised – are the foundations for building effective strategies to access and exercise power and authority, as well as the ability to challenge, critique and take appropriate action. The development of more collective and communal focused formulations, which reach out towards alternative, progressive social configurations and movements, might enable TCs once again to forge more revolutionary concepts and practices.

# Chronology of Key Events
# at Paddington Day Hospital

| | |
|---|---|
| 1962 | Paddington Day Hospital established. It is situated within three floors of an NHS building, known as the Paddington Clinic and Day Hospital. In 1974 the building is renamed the Paddington Centre for Psychotherapy. |
| Early 1960s | The consultant Basil Gregory introduces TC approach into the day hospital with the addition of key staff from the Henderson Hospital in 1965. |
| 1964–66 | Julian Goodburn is assistant registrar. |
| 1966–68 | Goodburn is senior registrar at the Tavistock Clinic, working closely with Henry Ezriel. |
| 1970 | Gregory leaves and on his recommendation is replaced by Goodburn as locum director in May 1970 who introduces more libertarian methods into the day hospital. |
| 1971–72 | Reorganisation threatens day hospital with closure/transfer and a 'Save Paddington Day Hospital', campaign is launched. |
| 25 Feb 1972 | Patients and staff take direct action and gatecrash a meeting of the Regional Hospital Board to discuss the proposed closure. |
| 3 March 1972 | Public meeting is organised by the action group called 'Madness: A Choice of Treatment' at Sidney Webb College. Speakers include David Ennals, Malcolm Pines, Julian Goodburn and Tony Garnett. Meeting is attended by between 700 and 900 people. |

| | |
|---|---|
| April 11<br>1972 | Group informed that transfer proposal has been abandoned. The proposed demonstration turns into a celebration with street play and folk-singing, with about 100 people attending. |
| Summer<br>1972 | Formation of The ATC (Association of Therapeutic Communities). The ATC is formed following a 'roundtable' of a select few leading senior professionals working in TCs, including Julian Goodburn. Paddington Day Hospital is one of the first ATC members and is reported to be the first non-residential TC in the UK. |
| 1973 | Despite disputes as to his suitability, Goodburn eventually given full consultant post as medical director. |
| 21 March<br>1973 | A public meeting which launches the Mental Patients Union is held at Paddington Day Hospital. The meeting is called 'Is Psychiatry Social Repression? The Case for a Mental Patients Union: a Meeting of Patients and Ex-Patients'. Over 150 people are reported to have attended, over 100 of whom are described as patients or ex-patients. |
| 1974–1976 | An all-day 'large group' into which people can move in and out at liberty gradually becomes the main forum and activity in the day hospital. Inspired by the work of Henry Ezriel, the theory of 'transference to the institution' is developed. |
| 8 January<br>1976 | Staff issue a letter to patients proposing the withdrawal of meals and travel reimbursements. |
| 11 January<br>1976 | About half the patient group sign a letter of complaint demanding an inquiry into the functioning of the day hospital and its lack of shared decision-making. |
| February to<br>September<br>1976 | First Inquiry into the functioning of Paddington Day Hospital (during 'the long hot summer' of 1976). |
| September<br>1976 | Inquiry report recommendations. |

| 5 October<br>1976 | Patients are not permitted copies of the Inquiry report from the Area Health Authority (AHA) so some of them set off the fire alarm in order to obtain copies while staff attend to the fire drill. |
|---|---|
| 12 October<br>1976 | Goodburn proposes to offer two distinct categories of treatment in the day hospital – one which fully complies with the inquiry recommendations and the other which continues his method. Patients may choose to attend the method they prefer. |
| 19 October<br>1976 | The AHA refuses Goodburn's proposal and insist that the inquiry's recommendations are met for *all* patients. |
| 4 November<br>1976 | The medical director is suspended for failing to meet the inquiry's recommendations in full. |
| January<br>1977 | New locum consultant is appointed (Richard Crocket) who tries to re-establish a working TC. In the meantime a legal disciplinary Inquiry is instituted into Goodburn's behaviour and conduct. |
| October<br>1977 | Following the inquiry report's recommendations, Goodburn is dismissed by the Area Health Authority. Whilst he is not struck off the professional medical register, in effect, if he were to continue working in the NHS he would be demoted to registrar status. The Minister of Health rejects his subsequent appeal for reinstatement. |
| 1978–1979 | Crocket is forced to wind down the day hospital and gradually discharge the patients. |
| 1979 | The Day Hospital is formally closed down. |

# References

Adorno, T.W., Frenkel-Brunswick, E., Levinson, D. and Sanford, R. (1982) *The Authoritarian Personality*. New York: Norton.

Ahlin, G. (1981) 'On "A Therapeutic Community is Terminated".' *Group Analysis XV*, 1, 233–234.

Alaszewski, A., Manthorpe, J. and Walsh, M. (1995) 'Risk: The Sociological View of Perception and Management.' *Nursing Times*, 22 November, 91, 47.

Allen, P.D. (1992) 'User Involvement in a Therapeutic Community.' *Therapeutic Communities 13*, 4, 253–263.

Anon (2000) Anonymous staff member's interview with Author (30 June 2000).

Armes, D. (2000) 'Enablement and Exploitation: The Contradictory Potential of Community Care Policy for Mental Health Service Users.' Unpublished Paper presented to the Social Policy Association 33rd Annual Conference, July 2000.

Ashbach, C. and Shermer, V. (eds) (1987) *Object Relations, the Self and the Group*. London: Routledge.

Asylum (2004) 'Special Edition: Women and Personality Disorder by Women at the Margins.' Asylum: The Magazine for Democratic Psychiatry *14*, 3.

Babiker, G. and Arnold, L. (1997) *The Language of Injury: Comprehending Self-mutilation*. Oxford: Blackwell.

Bangay, F. (1988) 'A CAPO tribute to Eric Irwin.' *Asylum 3*, 1, 6–11.

Barnes, M. and Berke, J. (1971) *Mary Barnes: Two Accounts of a Journey through Madness*. London: MacGibbon and Kee.

Barnes, M. and Bowl, R. (2001) *Taking Over The Asylum: Empowerment and Mental Health*. Basingstoke: Palgrave.

Barnes, M. and Scott, A. (1989) *Something Sacred: Conversations, Writings, Paintings*. London: Free Association Books.

Barnett, M. (1973) *People Not Psychiatry*. London: Allen and Unwin Ltd.

Baron, C. (1984a) 'The Social Organisation of a Therapeutic Community: A Contemporary Case Study.' PhD Thesis, London School of Economics.

Baron, C. (1984b) 'The Paddington Day Hospital: Crisis and Control in a Therapeutic Institution.' *International Journal of Therapeutic Communities 5*, 3, 157–170.

Baron, C. (1985) 'A reply to Richard Crocket.' *International Journal of Therapeutic Communities 6*, 2, 115–118.

Baron, C. (1987) *Asylum to Anarchy*. London: Free Association Books.

Basaglia, F. (1985) 'What is Psychiatry?' *International Journal of Mental Health 14*, 1–2, 42–51.

Basaglia, F. (1987) 'The Institution Negated.' In F. Basaglia (1987) in N. Scheper-Hughes and A.M. Lovell (eds) *Psychiatry Inside Out: Selected Writings of Franco Basaglia.* New York: Columbia University Press.

Bayer, Ronald (1987) *Homosexuality and American Psychiatry: The Politics of Diagnosis.* New Jersey: Princeton University Press.

Benn, S. (1972) 'Will Sir Keith Joseph wait post mortem to make the diagnosis or, should the Paddington Day Hospital be closed?' *World Medicine* 29 February 7, 11, 35–45.

Berke, J. (2003) 'The Right to be at Risk.' Paper given to the Critical Psychiatry Network Conference on The Limits of Psychiatry, 13 June 2003, London.

Bion, W.R. (1961) *Experiences in Groups and Other Papers.* London: Tavistock Publications.

Blackwell, D. (2000) 'And Everyone Shall have a Voice: The Political Vision of Pat de Mare.' *Group Analysis 33,* 1, 51–162.

Blackwell, D. (2002) 'The Politicisation of Group Analysis in the 21st Century.' *Group Analysis 35,* 1, 105–118.

Bloor, M.J. (1981) 'Therapeutic Paradox: The Patient Culture and the Formal Treatment Programme in a Therapeutic Community.' *British Journal of Medical Psychology 54,* 359–369.

Bloor, M. and McIntosh, J. (1990) 'Surveillance and Concealment: A Comparison of Techniques of Client Resistance, Therapeutic Communities and Health Visiting.' In N.P. McKeganey and S. Cunningham-Burley *Readings in Medical Sociology.* London: Routledge.

Bloor. M., McKeganey, N. and Fonkert, D. (1988) *One Foot in Eden: A Sociological Study of the Range of Therapeutic Community Practice.* London: Routledge.

Bola, J.R. and Mosher, L.R. (2003) 'Two Year Outcomes from The Soteria Project.' *Journal of Nervous and Mental Diseases 191,* 4, 219–229.

Bondi, L. and Burman, E. (2001) 'Women and Mental Health: A Feminist Review.' *Feminist Review 68,* 6–33.

Bott, P. (1975) 'A Therapeutic Community Meeting: Ingrebourne Centre.' *ATC Bulletin 17,* 14–21.

Bowen, M. and Staebler, G. (2002) 'A Living Testament to the Power of Anarchy: An Enquiry into Relations between a Therapeutic Community and its Social and Political Environment.' *Therapeutic Communities 23,* 1, 33–44.

Bracken, P. and Thomas, P. (2001) 'Post-psychiatry: A New Direction for Mental Health.' *British Medical Journal 322,* 724–727.

Bracken, P. and Thomas, P. (2005) *Post Psychiatry.* Oxford: Oxford University Press.

Brandon, D. (1991) *Innovation without Change? Consumer Power in Psychiatric Services.* London: Macmillan.

Breggin, P. (1979) *Electroshock: Its Brain-Disabling Effects.* New York: Springer.

Breggin, P. (1994) *Toxic Psychiatry.* New York: St Martin's Press.

Bridger, H. (1985) 'The Discovery of the Therapeutic Community: The Northfield Experiments.' In E. Trist and H. Murray (eds) (1990) *The Social Engagement of Social Science.* A Tavistock Anthology, Vol.1: The Socio-Psychological Perspective. London: Free Association Books.

Brown, T. and Hanvey, C. (1987) 'The Spirit of the Times: Ten Years after Case Con.' *Community Care*, 9 July, 18–19.

Burman, E. (1994) *Deconstructing Developmental Psychology*. London: Routledge.

Burman, E. (1996) 'Psychology Discourse Practice: From Regulation to Resistance.' In E. Burman, G. Aitken, P. Alldred, R. Allwood, T. Billington, B. Goldberg, A. Gordo Lopez, C. Heenan, D. Marks and S. Warner *Psychology Discourse Practice: From Regulation to Resistance*. London: Taylor and Francis.

Burman, E. (2001) 'Engendering Authority in the Group.' *Psychodynamic Counselling 7*, 3, 347–69.

Burston, D. (1996) *The Wing of Madness: The Life and Work of R.D. Laing*. Cambridge, Massachusetts and London: Harvard University Press.

Burton, M. (2000) 'Service Development and Social Change: The Role of Social Movements.' In C. Kagan (ed.) *Interpersonal Organisational Development Research Group, Occasional Papers No. 1/00 'Collective Action and Social Change'*. Manchester Metropolitan University, Department of Psychology and Speech Pathology.

Byrt, R. (1999) 'Nursing: The Importance of the Psychosocial Environment.' In P. Campling and R. Haigh (1999) *Therapeutic Communities: Past, Present and Future*. London: Jessica Kingsley Publishers.

Campbell, P. (1996) 'The History of the User Movement in the United Kingdom.' In T. Heller, J. Reynolds, R. Gomm, R. Muston and S. Pattison *Mental Health Matters: A Reader*. Buckingham: Open University Press.

Campbell, P. (1999) 'The Service User/Survivor Movement.' In C. Newnes, C. G. Holmes, C. Dunn (eds) *This is Madness: A Critical Look at The Future of Mental Health Services*. Ross on Wye, Herefordshire: PCCS Books.

Campling, P. (2001) 'Therapeutic Communities.' *Advances in Psychiatric Treatment 7*, 365–372.

Campling, P. and Haigh, R. (eds) (1999) *Therapeutic Communities: Past, Present and Future*. London: Jessica Kingsley Publishers.

Carroll, N. (1998) 'Interpretation, History and Narrative.' In B. Fay, P. Pomper and R.T. Vann (ed.) *History and Theory: Contemporary Readings*. Oxford: Blackwell.

Carter, D. (2001) 'Research and Survive: A Critical Question for Group Analysis.' *Group Analysis 35*, 1, 119–134.

Castel, R. (1991) 'From Dangerousness to Risk.' In G. Burchell, C. Gordon and P. Miller (eds) *The Foucault Effect: Studies in Governmentality*. London: Harvester Wheatsheaf.

Castel, R., Castel, F. and Lovell, A. (1982) *The Psychiatric Society*. New York: Columbia University Press.

Castillo, H. (2000) 'User Views on Personality Disorder: An Account of an Emancipatory Research Study about Personality Disorder.' *Mental Health Care*, October 2000.

Chamberlain, J. (1988) *On Our Own: Patient Controlled Alternatives to the Mental Health System*. London: Mind.

Chapman, G. (1986) 'Social Action Theory and Psychosocial Nursing.' In R. Kennedy, A. Heymans and L. Tischler (eds) *The Family as In-patient: Working with Families and Adolescents at the Cassel Hospital*. Free Association Books, London.

Chapman, G.E. (1988) 'Talk, Text and Discourse in a Therapeutic Community.' *International Journal of Therapeutic Communities 9*, 2, 75–87.

Chesler, P. (1972) *Women and Madness.* San Diego: Harvest, Harcourt Brace, Jovanovich.

Clark, D.H. (1965) 'The Therapeutic Community: Concept, Practice and Future.' *British Journal of Psychiatry 111*, 947–954.

Clarke, L. (2004) *The Time of the Therapeutic Community: People, Places and Events.* London: Jessica Kingsley Publishers.

Claytor, A. (1993) 'A Changing Faith? A History of Developments in Radical Critiques of Psychiatry since the 1960s', PhD thesis, University of Sheffield.

Cohen, L. (1969) 'Bird on a Wire', from *Songs From a Room.* Sony/ATV.

Coleman, R. and Smith, M. (1997) *Working with Voices – Victim to Victor.* Gloucester: Handsell Publications.

Cooklin, A. (1981) 'On "a Therapeutic Community is Terminated".' *Group Analysis XV*, 1, 47–48.

Cooper, A. (2001) 'The State of Mind We're In: Social Anxiety, Governance and the Audit Society.' *Psychoanalytic Studies 3*, 2/3, 349–362.

Cooper, B. (2003) 'Evidence-based Mental Health Policy: A Critical Appraisal.' *British Journal of Psychiatry 183*, 105–113.

Cooper, D. (1965) 'The Anti Hospital: An Experiment in Psychiatry.' *New Society*, 11 March 1965, 11–17.

Cooper, D. (1967) *Psychiatry and Anti-Psychiatry.* London: Tavistock Publications.

Cooper, D. (1980) *The Language of Madness.* London: Harmondsworth, Pelican.

Cooper, R. (1999) 'With the Best of Intentions.' Paper presented at the ATC Conference, September 1999.

Cooper, R., Heaton, J., and Oakley, C. (1994) *Thresholds between Philosophy and Psychoanalysis.* London: Free Association Books.

Copeman (1973) Copeman Newsletter No. 4, London.

Coppock, V. and Hopton, J. (2000) *Critical Perspectives on Mental Health.* London: Routledge.

Craib, I. (2001) 'Social Theory for Group Therapists.' *Group Analysis 34*, 1, 143–152.

Cresswell, M. (2004) 'Psychiatric Survivors' Knowledge and Testimonies of Self Harm.' Paper presented to 'Imaging Social Movements', the 2nd International Conference of the Social and Cultural Movements Group, Edge Hill College, UK, July 2004.

Crocket R. (1966) 'Authority and Permissiveness in the Psychotherapeutic Community: Theoretical Perspectives.' *American Journal of Psychotherapy 20*, 4, 669–76.

Crocket, R. (1978) 'Boundaries, Power and the Paddington Day Hospital: Vicissitudes of a Therapeutic Community.' Unpublished Paper, June 1978.

Crocket, R. (1985) 'On Claire Baron's Paper "The PDH: Crisis and Control in a Therapeutic Institution".' *International Journal Of Therapeutic Communities 6*, 2, 109–114.

Crossley, M. and Crossley, N. (2001) 'Patient Voices, Social Movements and the Habitus: How Psychiatric Survivors Speak Out.' *Social Science and Medicine 52*, 1477–1489.

Crossley, N. (1998) 'R.D. Laing and the British Anti-psychiatry Movement: A Socio-historical Analysis.' *Social Science and Medicine 47*, 877–899.

Crossley, N. (1999a) 'Fish, Field, Habitus and Madness: The First Wave Mental Health Users' Movement.' *British Journal of Sociology 50*, 4, 647–670.

Crossley, N. (1999b) 'Working Utopias and Social Movements: An Investigation using Case-study Materials from Radical Mental Health Movements in Britain.' *Sociology 33*, 4, 809–830.

Crossley, N. (2001) 'The Global Anti-corporate Movement: A Preliminary Analysis.' In C. Barker and M. Tyldesley (eds) *Alternative Futures and Popular Protest: Seventh International Conference*, 17–19 April 2001, Vol. 1, Manchester Metropolitan University.

Crozier, A. (1979) 'Attempts at Democracy.' In R.D. Hinshelwood and N. Manning *Therapeutic Communities: Reflections and Progress*. London: Routledge and Kegan Paul.

Curtis, T., Dellar, R., Esther, L. and Watson, B. (2000) *Mad Pride: A Celebration of Mad Culture*. London: Spare Change Books.

Dalal, F. (1998) *Taking the Group Seriously: Towards a Post-Foulkesian Group Analytic Theory*. London: Jessica Kingsley Publishers.

Davies, L. (2000) Interview with Author (8 February 2000).

Davis, A. (1996) 'Risk, Work and Mental Health.' In H. Kemshall and J. Pritchard (eds) *Good Practice in Risk Assessment and Risk Management*. London: Jessica Kingsley Publishers.

Davison, J. (2001) 'The Contribution of Group Analysis to the Democratic Therapeutic Community.' MSc Dissertation in Group Psychotherapy. Oxford Brookes University.

Donnelly, M. (1992) *The Politics of Mental Health in Italy*. London: Routledge.

Douglas, M. (1978) *Purity and Danger: An Analysis of the Concepts of Pollution and Taboo*. London: Routledge and Kegan Paul.

Douglas, M. (1992) *Risk and Blame: Essays in Cultural Theory*. London: Routledge.

Douglas, M. and Wildavsky, A. (1983) *Risk and Culture: An Essay on the Selection of Technological and Environmental Dangers*. Berkeley and Los Angeles: University of California Press.

Douieb, B. (2000) Interview with Author (8 February 2000).

Downs, J. (ed) (2001) Coping with Voices and Visions: A Guide to Helping People who Experience Hearing Voices, Seeing Visions, Tactile or Other Sensations. Manchester: Hearing Voices Network.

Dunford, R. and Palmer, I. (1998) 'Discourse, Organisations and Paradox.' In D. Grant, T. Keenoy and C. Oswick (eds) *Discourse and Organization*. London: Sage Publications.

Durkin, L. (1972a) 'Patient power – review of a protest.' *Social Work Today 3*, 15, 14.

Durkin, L. (1972b) 'Protest at Paddington Day Hospital.' *Rat Myth and Magic: A Political Critique of Psychology*, 56.

Durkin, L. (1973) 'Mental Patients' Union.' *Health and Social Service Journal*, 4 August 1973.

Durkin, L. and Douieb, B. (1975) 'The Mental Patients' Union.' In D. Jones and M. Mayo *Community Work Two*. London: Routledge and Kegan Paul.

Ellison, D. (1976) 'Reply to Mental Therapy Under the Microscope.' Article from *The Guardian* reprinted in the *ATC Newsletter 20*, 8–10.

Ennals, D. (1973) *Out of Mind*. London: Arrow Books.

Ernst, S. and Goodison, L. (1981) *In Our Own Hands: A Book of Self Help Therapy*. London: The Women's Press.

Esteva, G. (1999) 'The Zapatistas and people's power.' *Capital and Class 68*, 153–182.

Estroff, S. (1981) *Making it Crazy: An Ethnography of Psychiatric Clients in an American Community*. Berkeley and Los Angeles: University of California Press.

Ezriel, H. (1950) 'A Psychoanalytic Approach to Group Treatment.' *British Journal of Medical Psychology 150*, 23, 59–74.

Ezriel, H. (1952) 'Notes on Psychoanalytic Group Therapy: II. Interpretation and Research.' *Psychiatry 15*, 119–126.

Ezriel, H. (1959) 'The Role of Transference in Psychoanalysis and Other Approaches to Group Treatment.' *Acta Psychotherapeutica, Supplement 7*, 35–46.

Falzon, C. (1998) *Foucault and Social Dialogue: Beyond Fragmentation*. London: Routledge.

Fanon, F. (1967) *The Wretched of the Earth*. London: Harmondsworth, Penguin.

Fanon, F. (1986) *Black Skin, White Masks*. London: Pluto Press.

Fantasia, R. (1988) *Cultures of Solidarity: Consciousness, Action, and Contemporary Workers*. Berkeley: University of California Press.

Forbes, J. and Sashidharan, S.P. (1997) 'User Involvement in Services – Incorporation or Challenge?' *British Journal of Social Work 27*, 4, 481–98.

Foucault, M. (1971) *Madness & Civilization: A History of Insanity in the Age of Reason*. London: Tavistock Press.

Foucault, M. (1977) *Discipline & Punish: The Birth of the Prison*. London: Allen Lane.

Freeman, J. (1974) 'The Tyranny of Structurelessness.' In J. Freeman and C. Levine (1984) *Untying the Knot: Feminism, Anarchism and Organisation*. London: Dark Star Press and Rebel Press.

Freeman, J. (1999) 'On the Origins of Social Movements.' In J. Freeman and V. Johnson (eds) *Waves of Protest: Social Movements since the Sixties*. Maryland: Rowman and Littlefield.

Furedi, F. (1997) *Culture of Fear: Risk Taking and the Morality of Low Expectation*. London: Casell.

Giannichedda, M.G. (1989) 'Italy: 10 years of Reform.' *Asylum 3*, 3, 10–14.

Gibbs, L. and Gambrill, E. (2002) 'Evidence-based Practice: Counterarguments to Objections.' *Research on Social Work Practice 12*, 452–76.

Gillman, S.L. (1985) *Difference and Pathology: Stereotypes of Sexuality, Race and Madness*. New York: Cornell University Press.

Glennister, D. (2002) 'Thinking about Living Traditions: A Commentary upon Bowen and Staebler's "A Living Testament to the Power of Anarchy".' *Therapeutic Communities 23*, 1, 45–46.

Glynne, A. (2003) *Fish on a Hook*. Reel Madness Film Festival 2003, DFG Films, UK.

Goffman, E. (1961) *Asylums: Essays on the Social Situation of Mental Patients and Other Inmates.* London, Harmondsworth: Penguin.

Goodburn, J. (1972) 'A Unique Therapeutic Community.' *The Spectator* 18 March 1972, p.459.

Goodburn, J. (1976) 'Long Term Psychotherapy: The Concept of Transference to the Institution.' Unpublished paper, May 1976.

Goodburn, J. (1977) 'Paddington Day Hospital Inquiry.' In J. Cobb and F. Creed (eds) *Responsibility in Psychiatry, Part Three: Proceedings of a meeting of the Association of Psychiatrists in Training at the Institute of Psychiatry,* London, 8 February 1977.

Goodburn, J. (1986) 'Paddington Day Hospital or the Psyche Misunderstood: Implications for Therapeutic Communities, Psychotherapy and Psychoanalysis.' *International Journal of Therapeutic Communities 7,* 1, 57–66.

Goodburn, J. (2000) Interview with Author (28–30 January 2000).

Gordon, P. (2001) 'Psychoanalysis and Racism: The Politics of Defeat.' *Race and Class 42,* 4, 17–34.

Grant, D., Keenoy, T. and Oswick, C. (eds) (1998) *Discourse and Organisation.* London: Sage Publications.

Gregory, B.A.J.C. (1968) 'The Day Hospital as a Therapeutic Community.' *Group Analysis 1,* 2, 71–73.

Grunberg, S. (1979) 'The Implications of the Erosion of Authority in a Therapeutic Community.' Paper given at ATC Conference, September 1979.

Habermas, J. (1987) *The Theory of Communicative Action: Vol. 2.* Polity Press: Cambridge.

Haddon, B. (1973) Untitled article in *ATC Newsletter 7,* 4.

Haddon, B. (1979) 'Political Implications of Therapeutic Communities.' In R.D. Hinshelwood and N. Manning *Therapeutic Communities: Reflections and Progress.* London: Routledge and Kegan Paul.

Haigh, R. (1999) 'The Quintessence of a Therapeutic Community: Five Universal Qualities.' In P. Campling and R. Haigh *Therapeutic Communities: Past, Present and Future.* London: Jessica Kingsley Publishers.

Haigh, R. (2004) 'Charismatic Ideas.' The Maxwell Jones Lecture, 12 September 2004.

Hall, M. (1972) 'A Patients' Commune in Paddington.' *British Hospital Journal and Social Service Review,* 16 December 1972, 2813–2814.

Hall, M. (1973) 'The Fordingly Commune Project.' *ATC Newsletter 11,* 1–10.

Hall, M. (1979) 'The Closure of Paddington Day Hospital.' Paper presented to the ATC Conference 1979.

Harris, C. and Barraclough, B. (1997) 'Suicide as an Outcome for Mental Disorders.' *British Journal of Psychiatry 170,* 205–228.

Harrison, S. (1998) 'Evidence-based Medicine in the National Health Service: Towards the History of a Policy.' In R. Skelton and V. Williamson (eds) *Fifty Years of the National Health Service: Continuities and Discontinuities in Health Policy.* Brigton: University of Brighton.

Herbert, H. (1976) 'Mental Therapy under the Microscope.' *The Guardian,* 25 June.

Hervey, N. (1986) 'Advocacy or Folly: The Alleged Lunatics Friends Society 1845–63.' *Medical History 30,* 245–271.

Hill, C., Martin, J. and Roberts, A. (1975) *A Directory of the Side Effects of Psychiatric Drugs.* MPU, October 1975.

Hinshelwood, R.D. (1977) 'Comment on Paddington Day Hospital Inquiry.' *ATC Newsletter* No. 21, February 1977, p.59.

Hinshelwood, R.D. (1979) 'A Community's Death and its Dynamics.' Paper to ATC Conference, September 1979.

Hinshelwood, R.D. (1980) 'Seeds of Disaster.' *International Journal of Therapeutic Communities 1,* 181–188.

Hinshelwood, R.D. (1987) *What Happens in Groups? Psychoanalysis, the Individual and the Community.* London: Free Association Books.

Hinshelwood, R.D. (1996) 'Communities and their Health.' *Therapeutic Communities 17,* 3, 173–182.

Hinshelwood, R.D. (1999) 'Psychoanalytic Origins and Today's Work: The Cassel Heritage.' In P. Campling and R. Haigh (eds) *Therapeutic Communities: Past, Present and Future.* London: Jessica Kingsley Publishers.

Hinshelwood, R.D. (2000) Personal communication with Author (June/July 2000).

Hinshelwood, R.D. (2002) Personal communication with Author (September 2002).

Hinshelwood, R.D. and Grunberg, S. (1979) 'The Large Group Syndrome.' In R.D. Hinshelwood and N. Manning *Therapeutic Communities: Reflections and Progress.* London: Routledge and Kegan Paul.

Hinshelwood, R.D. and Manning, N. (1979) *Therapeutic Communities: Reflections and Progress.* London: Routledge and Kegan Paul.

Hobson, R.F. (1979) 'The Messianic Community.' In R.D. Hinshelwood and N. Manning *Therapeutic Communities: Reflections and Progress.* London: Routledge and Kegan Paul.

Hochmann, J. (1985) 'Psychiatric Deinstitutionalisation in Italy: A Neighbour's Viewpoint.' *International Journal of Mental Health 14,* 1–2, 184–194.

Holland, S. (1992) 'From Social Abuse to Social Action: A Neighbourhood Psychotherapy and Social Action Project from Women.' In J.M. Ussher and P. Nicholson (eds) *Gender Issues in Clinical Psychology.* London: Routledge.

Hopton, J. (2000) 'The Future of Therapeutic Communities in Adult Mental Health Services.' Report from research funded by Nuffield Foundation.

Hopton, J. (2001) 'Therapeutic Communities and "Personality Disorders".' Unpublished paper.

Hughes, J. (1986) 'A Short Talk on the History of Mental Patients Movements.' Unpublished paper.

Irwin, E., Mitchell, L., Durkin, L. and Douieb, B. (2000) 'The Need for a Mental Patients' Union.' In T. Curtis, R. Dellar, E. Leslie and B. Watson (eds) *Mad Pride: A Celebration of Mad Culture.* London: Spare Change Books.

Jablensky, A. (1992) 'Schizophrenia: Manifestations, Incidence and Course in Different Cultures: A World Health Organisation Ten-country Study.' *Psychological Medicine Suppl, 20,* 1–95.

Jacoby, R. (1975) *Social Amnesia: A Critique of Conformist Psychology from Adler to Jung.* Boston: Beacon Press.

Jacoby, R. (1983) *The Repression of Psychoanalysis: Otto Fenichel and the Political Freudians.* Chicago: University of Chicago Press.

Jenkins. K. (1991) *Re-thinking History.* London: Routledge.

Jenner, N. (2000) Interview with Author (16 May 2000).

Johnstone, L. (2000) *Users and Abusers of Psychiatry: A Critical Look at Psychiatric Practice.* London: Routledge.

Jones, M. (1968) *Beyond the Therapeutic Community: Social Learning and Social Psychiatry.* New Haven: Yale University Press.

Jong, E. (1974) *Fear of Flying.* New York: Granada Publications.

Kavalier, F. (1972) 'Who Decides, Who Rules, Who Cares if Paddington Day Hospital Dies an Early Death?' *Nursing Times,* 27 April, 490–492.

KCWAHA (1976) Kensington and Chelsea and Westminster Area Health Authority Report of the Committee of Enquiry Concerning the Day Hospital at the Paddington Centre for Psychotherapy (September 1976).

Keenoy, T., Oswick, C. and Grant, D. (1997) 'Organizational Discourses: Text and Context.' *Organization 4,* 2, 147–57.

Kendall, T. (1996) 'Trieste: The Current Situation.' Paper presented to the Third International Conference on Psychosis 'Integrating the Inner and Outer Worlds', University of Essex, September 1996.

Kennard, D. (1979) 'Limiting Factors: The Setting, The Staff, the Patients.' In R.D. Hinshelwood and N. Manning *Therapeutic Communities: Reflections and Progress.* London: Routledge and Kegan Paul.

Kennard, D. (1982) 'On "A Therapeutic Community is Terminated".' *Group Analysis XV,* 2, August 1982, 174–175.

Kennard, D. (1986) 'From a Movement to a Method.' *International Journal of Therapeutic Communities 7,* 4, 207–209.

Kennard, D. (1991) 'The Therapeutic Community Impulse: A Recurring Democratic Tendency in Troubled Times.' *Changes 1,* 33–43.

Kennard, D. (1994) 'The Future Revisited: New Frontiers for Therapeutic Communities.' *Therapeutic Communities 15,* 2, 107–113.

Kennard, D. (1998) *An Introduction to Therapeutic Communities.* London: Jessica Kingsley Publishers.

Kotowicz, Z. (1997) *R.D. Laing and the Paths of Anti-Psychiatry.* London: Routledge.

Kreeger, L. (1970) 'Problems of the Therapeutic Community.' *Group Analysis 3,* 149–155.

Kreeger, L. (1981) 'On "A Therapeutic Community is Terminated".' *Group Analysis XV,* 1, 231–232.

Laing, R.D. (1960) *The Divided Self: An Existential Study in Sanity and Madness.* London: Tavistock Press.

Laing, R.D. (1968) 'Metanoia: Some Experiences at Kingsley Hall.' Reprinted in H.W. Ruitenbeek (ed.) (1972) *Going Crazy.* New York: Bantam Books.

Laing, R.D. and Esterson, A. (1958) 'The Collusive Functioning of Pairing in Analytic Groups.' *British Journal of Medical Psychology 31,* 117–23.

Lawson, M. (1999) Interview with Author (24 September 1999).

Lees, J. (1999) 'Research: The Importance of Asking Questions.' In P. Campling and R. Haigh (eds) *Therapeutic Communities: Past, Present and Future.* London: Jessica Kingsley Publishers.

Lees, J.D. and Manning, N. (1984) 'Problems on the Psychology of Personality and Environment, and some Marxist Solutions.' *International Journal of Therapeutic Communities 5*, 1, 6–24.

Leff, J. (1992) 'The International Pilot Study of Schizophrenia: Five-year Follow-up Findings.' *Psychological Medicine 22*, 131–145.

Leifer, R. (1969) *In the Name of Psychiatry.* New York: Science House.

Leitner, M. (1999) 'Pathologising as a Way of Dealing with Conflicts and Dissent in the Psychoanalytic Movement.' *Free Associations 7*, 3, 459–483.

Lemlij, M., Mulvany, S. and Nagle, C.J. (1979) Unpublished full paper presented to the RCP, November 1979.

Lemlij, M., Mulvany, S. and Nagle, C.J. (1982) 'A Therapeutic Community is Terminated.' *Group Analysis XV*, 3, 216–219.

Lindow, V. (1994) *Self-help Alternatives to Mental Health Services.* London: Mind.

Lomas, P. (1987) *The Limits of Interpretation: What's Wrong with Psychoanalysis?* London: Harmondsworth, Penguin.

Lougher, L. (2000) Interview with Author (March/April 2000).

Mahony, N. (1979) 'My Stay and Change at the Henderson Therapeutic Community.' In R.D. Hinshelwood and N. Manning (1979) *Therapeutic Communities: Reflections and Progress.* London: Routledge and Kegan Paul.

Main, T. (1983) 'The Concept of the Therapeutic Community: Variations and Vicissitudes.' In M. Pines (ed.) *The Evolution of Group Analysis.* London: Routledge and Kegan Paul.

Manning, N. (1979) 'The Politics of Survival: The Role of Research in the Therapeutic Community.' In R.D. Hinshelwood and N. Manning *Therapeutic Communities: Reflections and Progress.* London: Routledge and Kegan Paul.

Manning, N. (1989) *The Therapeutic Community Movement: Charisma and Routinization.* London: Routledge.

Manning, N. (1991) 'Maxwell Jones and the Therapeutic Community Movement: A Sociological Review.' *International Journal of Therapeutic Communities 12*, 2–3.

Margison, F. (1992) 'The Poet as Hero: The Ethics of Returning Men to War.' *Changes 10*, 2, 108–114.

Martin, G. (2001) 'Social Movements, Welfare and Social Policy: A Critical Analysis.' *Critical Social Policy 21*, 3, 361–383.

Martin, J.P. (1984) *Hospitals in Trouble.* Oxford: Blackwell.

McLaughlin, T. (2000) 'Psychology and Mental Health Politics: A Critical History of the Hearing Voices Network.' PhD Thesis, Manchester Metropolitan University.

McLean, A. (1995) 'Empowerment and the Psychiatric Consumer/Ex-patient Movement in the United States: Contradictions, Crisis and Change.' *Social Science and Medicine 40*, 8, 1053–107.

Melucci, A. (1989) *Nomads of the Present.* London: Hutchinson.

Melucci, A. (1995) 'The Process of Collective Identity.' In H. Johnston and B. Klandermans (eds) *Social Movements and Culture.* University College, London.

Melucci, A. (1996) *Challenging Codes: Collective Action in the Information Age.* Cambridge: Cambridge University Press.

Millard, D.W. (1985) 'Editorial: The Paddington Events: A Philosophical Reflection.' *International Journal of Therapeutic Communities 6,* 2, 67–70.

Mitchell, S. (1988) *Relational Concepts in Psychoanalysis.* Cambridge: Harvard University Press.

Mitchie, S. (1980) 'A Therapeutic Community in Cuba.' *International Journal of Therapeutic Communities 1,* 2, 92–99.

Moncrieff, J., Hopker, S. and Thomas, P. (2005) 'Psychiatry and the Pharmaceutical Industry: Who Pays the Piper? A Perspective from the Critical Psychiatry Network.' *Psychiatric Bulletin 29,* 84–85.

Mosher, L.R. (1991a) 'In Memoriam: R.D. Laing. An Anti-psychiatrist's Contribution to Contemporary Psychiatry.' *International Journal of Therapeutic Communities 12,* 1, 43–51.

Mosher, L.R. (1991b) 'Soteria: A Therapeutic Community for Psychotic Persons.' *International Journal of Therapeutic Communities 12,* 1, 53–67.

Mosher L.R. (1999) 'Soteria and Other Alternatives to Acute Hospitalization: A Personal and Professional Review.' *Journal of Nervous and Mental Diseases 187,* 142–149.

Mosher, L., Hendrix, V. and Fort, D. (2004) *Soteria: Through Madness to Deliverance.* Philadelphia: Xlibris Corporation.

Mosher, L.R., Vallone, R. and Menn A.Z. (1995) 'The Treatment of Acute Psychosis without Neuroleptics: Six-week Psychopathology Outcome Data from the Soteria Project.' *International Journal of Social Psychiatry 41,* 157–173.

MPU (1972) 'The Need for a Mental Patient Union.' Unpublished pamphlet, circulated 1972.

MPU (1974) *Mental Patients' Union News* No. 3, February 1974.

Mullan, B. (1995) *Mad to be Normal: Conversations with R.D. Laing.* London: Free Association Books.

Mullan, B. (ed.) (1997) *R.D. Laing: Creative Destroyer.* London: Cassell.

Neal, S. (1998) 'Embodying Black Madness, Embodying White Femininity: Populist (Re) presentations and Public Policy – The Case of Christopher Clunis and Jayne Zito.' *Sociological Research Online 3,* 4.

Nehls, N. (1999) 'Borderline Personality Disorder: The Voice of Patients.' *Research in Nursing & Health 22,* 285–293.

Newman, F. (1991) *The Myth of Psychology.* New York: Castillo.

Newnes, C., Holmes, G. and Dunn, C. (eds) (1999) *This is Madness: A Critical Look at The Future of Mental Health Services.* Ross on Wye, Herefordshire: PCCS Books.

Newnes, C., Holmes, G. and Dunn, C. (eds) (2001) *This is Madness Two: Critical Perspectives on Mental Health Services.* Ross on Wye, Herefordshire: PCCS Books.

Nitsun, M. (1996) *The Anti-Group: Destructive Forces in the Group and their Creative Potential.* London: Routledge.

Nitzgen, D. (1999) 'From Demand to Desire: What Do We Offer When We Offer Group Analytic Training?' *Group Analysis 32*, 2, 227–239.

Norman, A.P. (1998) 'Telling It Like It Was: Historical Narratives on Their Own Terms.' In B. Fay, P. Pomper and R.T. Vann (eds) *History and Theory: Contemporary Readings.* Oxford: Blackwell.

Norton, K. (1996) 'A Culture of Enquiry: Its Preservation and Loss.' In B. Dolan (ed.) *Perspectives on Henderson Hospital.* Surrey: Henderson Hospital.

Oakley, C. (1989) 'Review of Asylum to Anarchy.' *Free Associations 15*, 108–125.

O'Hagan, M. (1993) *Stopovers on my Way Home from Mars: Reflective Journey through the Psychiatric Survivor Movement in the USA, Britain and the Netherlands.* New Zealand: Self Publication.

Paddington Mercury (1972) 'Hundreds Fight To Save Day Hospital', 10 March 1972, p.1.

Paddington Mercury (1976a) 'Paddington Hospital Director Replies to Treatment Critics', 22 October 1976, p.1.

Paddington Mercury (1976b) 'Paddington Hospital Director Suspended', 12 November 1976, p.36.

Papeschi, R. (1985) 'The Denial of the Institution: A Critical Review of Basaglia's writings.' *British Journal of Psychiatry 146*, 247–254.

Parker, I. (1997) *Psychoanalytic Culture: Psychoanalytic Discourse in Western Society.* London: Sage.

Parker, I., Georgaca, E., Harper, D., McLaughlin, T. and Stowell-Smith, M. (1995) *Deconstructing Psychopathology.* London: Sage.

Parton, N. (2003) 'Rethinking Professional Practice. The Contributions of Social Constructionism and the Feminist Ethics of Care.' *British Journal of Social Work 33*, 1, 1–16.

Pembroke, L. (1998) 'Self Harm: A Personal Story.' *Mental Health Practice,* 12 October, 2, 20–24.

Perceval, J. (1961) *Perceval's Narrative: A Patient's Account of his Psychosis* (edited by G. Bateson). Palo Alto: Stanford University Press.

Perrow, C. (1965) 'Hospitals: Technology, Structure, Goals.' In J.D. March (ed.) *Handbook of Organisations.* Chicago: Rand McNally.

Pilgrim, D. (2001) 'Disordered Personalities and Disordered Concepts.' *Journal of Mental Health 10*, 253–265.

Pines, M. (1999) 'Forgotten Pioneers: The Unwritten History of the Therapeutic Community Movement.' *Therapeutic Communities 20*, 1, 23–42.

Pirkis, J. and Burgess, P. (1998) 'Suicide and Recency of Health Care Contacts.' *British Journal of Psychiatry 173*, 462–474.

Plunket, E., Main, T., Williams, T. and Crozier, A. (1976) 'A Visit to the Paddington' *ATC Newsletter 20*, 10–14.

Podvoll, E.M. (1991) *The Seduction of Madness: A Compassionate Approach to Recovery at Home.* London: Century.

Pope, C. (2003) 'Resisting Evidence: The Study of Evidence-based Medicine as a Contemporary Movement.' *Health: An Interdisciplinary Journal for the Study of Health, Illness and Medicine 7*, 3, 267–282.

Proctor, G. (2002) *The Dynamics of Power in Counselling and Psychotherapy: Ethics, Politics and Practice.* Ross on Wye, Herefordshire: PCCS Books.

Pullen, G. (1999) 'Schizophrenia: Hospital Communities for the Severely Disturbed.' In P. Campling and R. Haigh (eds) *Therapeutic Communities: Past, Present and Future.* London: Jessica Kingsley Publishers.

Ramon, S. (ed.) (1988) *Psychiatry in Transition.* London: Pluto Press.

Ramon, S. (1989) 'The Impact of the Italian Psychiatric Reforms on North American and British professionals.' *The International Journal of Social Psychiatry 35*, 1, 120–7.

Rapoport, R. N. (1960) *Community as Doctor.* London: Tavistock.

Rappaport, J. (1986) 'In Praise of Paradox: A Social Policy of Empowerment over Prevention.' In E. Seidman and J. Rappaport (eds) *Redefining Social Problems.* New York: Plenum Press.

Rawlings, W.B. (1980) 'Everyday Therapy.' PhD Thesis, University of Manchester.

Rawlinson, D. (1999) 'Group Analytic Ideas: Extending the Group Matrix to Therapeutic Communities.' In P. Campling and R. Haigh (eds) *Therapeutic Communities: Past, Present and Future.* London: Jessica Kingsley Publishers.

Reder, P. (1976) 'The PDH – Theory and Practice.' Unpublished Paper dated March 1976.

Reich, W. (1975) *Listen Little Man!* London: Harmondsworth, Pelican.

Roberts, J. (1982) 'On "A Therapeutic Community is Terminated".' *Group Analysis XV*, 2, 175–6.

Robinson, S. (1994) 'Life after Death.' *Therapeutic Communities 15*, 2, 77–86.

Rogers, A. and Pilgrim, D. (1991) 'Pulling Down Churches: Accounting for the British Mental Health Users' Movement.' *Sociology of Health and Illness 13*, 29–48.

Romme, M. and Escher, S. (2000) *Making Sense of Voices – A guide for Professionals who Work with Voice Hearers.* London: Mind Publications.

Rose, G. (1993) *Feminism and Geography: The Limits of Geographical Knowledge.* Minneapolis: University of Minnesota Press.

Rose, N. (1986) 'Psychiatry: the Discipline of Mental Health.' In P. Miller and N. Rose (eds) *The Power of Psychiatry.* Cambridge: Polity Press.

Rose, N. (1996) 'Psychiatry as a Political Science: Advanced Liberalism and the Administration of Risk.' *History of the Human Sciences 9*, 1–23.

Rosen, I. (1996) 'Along the Way.' Unpublished autobiography.

Routledge, P. (2001) 'Convergent Space and the Fluidity of Networks.' In 'Alternative Futures and Popular Protest': Seventh International Conference, 17–19 April 2001, Vol. 11. Edited by C. Barker and M. Tyldesley. Manchester Metropolitan University.

Rowbotham, S., Segal, L. and Wainwright, H. (1980) *Beyond the Fragments: Feminism and the Making of Socialism.* London: Merlin.

Samuels, A. (1993) *The Political Psyche.* London: Routledge.

Sandison, R. (1982) 'On "a Therapeutic Community is Terminated".' *Group Analysis XV*, 2, 176–8.

Scheper-Hughes, N. and Lovell, A. M. (1987) *Psychiatry Inside Out: Selected Writings of Franco Basaglia (1924–1980)*. New York: Columbia University Press.

Sedgwick, P. (1982) *Psychopolitics*. London: Pluto Press.

Seeger, P. (1996) 'A Concise Political History of the User Movement.' *Asylum 9*, 4, 12–13.

Sharp, V. (1975) *Social Control in the Therapeutic Community*. Hants: Saxon House.

Showalter, E. (1987) *The Female Malady: Women, Madness and English Culture 1830–1980*. London: Virago Press.

Sigal, C. (1976) *Zone of the Interior*. Toronto: Popular Library.

Small, S. (undated) 'Keep Madness at Bay – Keep the Patients Down at Paddington Day.' In *Copeman 2*, 6–9.

Smith, B. (1971) Unpublished leaflet circulated during Paddington Day Hospital protest.

Smith, J. (1972) 'Network.' *Social Work Today 3*, 2, 7.

Spandler, H. (1992) 'To Make an Army out of Illness: a History of the Socialist Patients' Collective Heidelberg 1970–2.' *Asylum 6*, 4, 3–16.

Spandler, H. (2001) 'Julian, not Adrian, Julian Goodburn: An Appreciation.' *Therapeutic Communities 22*, 4, 335–337.

Spandler, H. (2002) *Asylum to Action: Paddington Day Hospital, Therapeutic Communities and Beyond*. PhD thesis, October 2002, Department of Psychology and Speech Pathology, Manchester Metropolitan University.

Spandler, H. (2004) 'Friend or Foe? Towards a Critical Assessment of Direct Payments.' *Critical Social Policy 24*, 2, 187–209.

Spector, R. (2001) 'Is there Racial Bias in Clinicians' Perceptions of the Dangerousness of Psychiatric Patients? A Review of the Literature.' *Journal of Mental Health 10*, 1, 5–15.

SPK (1972) 'To Make an Army out of Illness.' First English Draft of SPK document 'SPK: Aus der Krankheit eine Waffe machen'. Written by the Socialist Patients Collective of Heidelberg University. Munich: Trikont Verlag.

SPK (1993) *Turn Illness into a Weapon*. Heidelberg: KRRIM Publications.

Stanley, N. and Manthorpe, J. (2004) *The Age of the Inquiry: Learning and Blaming in Health and Social Care*. London: Routledge.

Sturdy, C. (1987) 'Questioning the Sphinx: An Experience of Working in a Women's Organisation.' In S. Ernst and M. Maguire (eds) *Living with the Sphinx: Papers from the Women's Therapy Centre*. London: Women's Press.

Sugerman, B. (1975) 'Reluctant Converts: Social Control, Socialisation and Adaptation in Therapeutic Communities.' In R. Wallis (ed.) *Sectarianism*. New York: John Wiley and Sons.

Szmukler, G. (2001) 'A New Mental Health (and Public Protection) Act: Risk Wins in the Balance between Providing Care and Controlling Risk.' *British Medical Journal 322*, 2–3.

Szmukler, G. and Holloway, F. (2000) 'Reform of the Mental Health Act: Health or Safety?' *British Journal of Psychiatry 177*, 196–200.

Thomas, P.B. (2000) Interview with Author (28–30 January 2000).

Thompson, J. (1995) *User Involvement in Mental Health: The Limits of Consumerism, the Risks of Marginalisation and the Need for a Critical Approach.* University of Hull, Centre for Systems Studies, Research Memorandum No. 8.

Tucker, S. (ed.) (2000) *A Therapeutic Approach to Care in the Community Dialogue and Dwelling.* London: Jessica Kingsley Publishers.

Tucker, S. (2001) 'Psychosis and the Therapeutic Community: Beyond the User Movement? *Therapeutic Communities 22*, 3, 233–47.

Van de Graaf, W. (1989a) 'The CAPO interview: with Eric Irwin and Frank Bangay.' *Asylum 3*, 3, 4–8.

Van de Graaf, W. (1989b) 'The CAPO Interview: with Eric Irwin and Frank Bangay: Part 2.' *Asylum 4*, 1, 5–8.

Van den Langenberg, S. and de Natris, P. (1985) 'A Narrow Escape from the Magic Mountain?' *International Journal of Therapeutic Communities 6*, 2, 91–101.

Venn, C. (1992) 'Subjectivity, Ideology and Difference: Recovering Otherness.' In *Competing Glances: a Journal of Culture/Theory/Politics 16*, 40–61.

Waitzkin, H. and Waterman, B. (1974) *The Exploitation of Illness in Capitalist Society.* Indianapolis: Bobbs-Merrill Co.

Walker, K., Burman, E. and Gowrisunkur, J. (2002) 'Counting Black Sheep: Contextualising Therapeutic Relations.' *Psychodynamic Practice 8*, 1, 55–73.

Walkerdine, V. and Lucey, H. (1989) *Democracy in the Kitchen: Regulating Mothers and Socialising Daughters.* London: Virago Press.

Ward, J. (1972) 'A Victorious Protest.' *Socialist Commentary*, August, 17–18.

Warner, R. (1994) *Recovery from Schizophrenia; Psychiatry and Political Economy.* London: Routledge.

Weaver, A. (1962) 'The Work of David Wills.' *Anarchy: A Journal of Anarchist Ideas 15*, 29–138.

White, H. (1986) 'Historical Pluralism.' *Critical Inquiry 12*, 480–493.

White, H. (1996) 'Storytelling: Historical and Ideological.' In R. Newman (ed.) *Centuries' Ends, Narrative Means.* Stanford University Press, Stanford: California.

White, H. (1999) 'History as Fulfilment.' Interdisciplinary Scholarly Network Keynote Address. (12 November 1999). http://www.Tulane.edu/~isn/hwkeynote.htm.

Whiteley, S. (1979) 'Progress and Reflection.' In R.D. Hinshelwood and N. Manning (eds) *Therapeutic Communities: Reflections and Progress.* London: Routledge and Kegan Paul.

Whiteley, S. (1980) 'The Henderson Hospital: A Community Study.' *International Journal of Therapeutic Communities 1*, 1, 38–58.

Whiteley, S. (1982) 'On "a Therapeutic Community is Terminated".' *Group Analysis XV*, 3, 235–6.

Whiteley, S. (1988) 'Book Review: Claire Baron, Asylum to Anarchy.' *Group Analysis 21*, 4, 371–372.

Winship G. (1995) 'Patient Empowerment: Individualism and Collectivism.' *Therapeutic Communities 16*, 2, 113–116.

Winship, G. (1997) 'Democracy in Psychiatric Settings: Collectivism vs. Individualism.' In P. Barker and B. Davidson (eds) *Ethical Dilemmas in Psychiatric Nursing.* London: Arnold.

Winship, G. and Haigh, R. (1999) *Towards a Communitarian Manifesto: The Third Way and the Public Therapeutic Community.* Unpublished discussion document.

Winship, G. and Haigh, R. (2000) 'Public Mental Health and the New Therapeutic Community.' *Therapeutic Communities 21*, 1, 47–53.

Winship, G. (2001) 'From Movement to Method to Maxim.' *The Joint Newsletter: The Joint Newsletter of the Association of Therapeutic Communities, the Charterhouse Group of Therapeutic Communities, and the Planned Environment Therapy Trust 3*, 10.

Winship, G. and Pines, M. (1996) 'Malcolm Pines interviewed by Gary Winship.' *Therapeutic Communities 17*, 2, 117–122.

Wodak, R. (1996) *Disorders of Discourse.* London: Longman.

Zeitlyn, B.B. (1967) 'The Therapeutic Community: Fact or Fantasy.' *British Journal of Psychiatry 113*, 1083–1086.

# Subject Index

Note: Paddington is used as an abbreviation for Paddington Day Hospital.

# Author Index